The Paranormal World of Paul McKenna

by the same author

THE HYPNOTIC WORLD OF PAUL MCKENNA
HYPNOTIC SECRETS

The Paranormal World of Paul McKenna

Paul McKenna
With Giles O'Bryen

faber and faber
LONDON · BOSTON

First published in 1997
by Faber and Faber Limited
3 Queen Square London WC1N 3AU

Photoset by Parker Typesetting Service, Leicester
Printed in England by Mackays of Chatham PLC, Chatham, Kent

A CIP record for this book
is available from the British Library
ISBN 0–571–19245–9

10 9 8 7 6 5 4 3 2

Contents

List of Plates   vi

Introduction   vii

1 Ghosts   1

2 UFOs   24

3 Psychic Detectives   57

4 Telepathy   75

5 Psychokinesis   104

6 Healing   130

7 Superhumans   151

8 The Future   162

Sources of Further Information   165

Further Reading   172

Index   180

List of Plates

1 Paul McKenna (Carlton Pictures)

2 Eddie Burks (Carlton Pictures)

3 Leo May (Carlton Pictures)

4 Nella Jones (Carlton Pictures)

5 Albert Ignatenko (Carlton Pictures)

6 UFO (Lee and Britt Elders © Genesis III)

7 Mutilated steer (Linda Moulton Howe)

8 Area 51

9 Bob Lazar (Fortean Picture Library)

10 Joe McMoneagle (Carlton Pictures)

11 Silba Knight (Carlton Pictures)

12 Valeri Lavrinenko (Carlton Pictures)

Introduction

The paranormal may be defined as those phenomena which can be proved to exist, but which science cannot yet explain.

I've travelled the world to witness strange and marvellous happenings – investigating UFOs, ghosts, mystics and psychics – and everything I see seems to open up a new realm of fantastic possibilities. My own speciality is hypnosis, and learning how to make the best use of the hidden or underused abilities of the human mind, but I am fascinated by any and all evidence of what have come to be known as 'paranormal phenomena'.

In this book I want to tell some of the truly wonderful stories I came across during my researches which, for various reasons, we did not feature in either of the TV series. To those whose curiosity was aroused by some of the amazing things they did see on TV, I also want to offer some background material which I hope they will find as fascinating and compelling as I do.

It is not my intention here to play the scientific investigator and to prove that the events described really happened – or otherwise. To prove things scientifically is a long and rigorous process that undoubtedly has an important part to play in exploring paranormal phenomena, but I will leave it to others to pursue this avenue of enquiry. Of course I have exercised common sense and discernment in deciding whether someone is genuine, or is trying to hoodwink people, or is deluded, and I have concentrated on phenomena which are demonstrably real – and which would be extraordinarily difficult to fake. But that doesn't mean I have gone round exhaustively unravelling every part of the process in order to try to pick holes in it. The fact is that there are plenty of remarkable capabilities to explore without delving into the outer reaches of human fantasy; and, though scientists are often wary of admitting it, there are plenty of 'improbable' events that have been replicated under test conditions and proved 'real', but which orthodox science simply cannot explain. These are the subject of this book.

For this reason, if for no other, I have tried to remain open to what people have told me, and not to react with instant scepticism to anything that seems out of the ordinary – even though it is often easier to dismiss than to accept. Science doesn't have all the answers, and no sensible scientist would claim that it does. Even the most sceptical scientists agree that this area should be investigated.

Besides, many of the most astounding abilities and effects I have witnessed are no different in kind from many everyday abilities that we take for granted. For example, we all know, and research suggests, that a person's 'will to live' greatly affects their chances of survival in cases of life-threatening illness or injury, and that on balance someone who thinks positively about themselves and their ability to get better will recover more quickly than someone who is full of doom and gloom about their prospects. That is a simple example of the ability of the mind to influence the body – similar to the same ability exhibited by healers and practitioners of many psychic skills. Again, it is common knowledge to sports men and women that by following the advice of psychologists and learning to focus attention in particular ways, players can greatly enhance their performance, and also endure pain from injury that would have them hobbling in agony to the nearest armchair if suffered outside the sporting arena. The very same psychological concepts – developed to an astonishing degree – are what enable the Shaolin monks to perform feats of strength and endurance so astonishing that many believe they must be illusory. Yet again, most people have experienced that uncomfortable prickling sensation at the back of the neck which means that someone is staring at them – and very often they have swung round to find that their 'intuition' was correct. What kind of power or energy is at work here? And if we could identify and develop it into a proper skill, what dazzling feats of perception might we be able to achieve? All this suggests that we may already be familiar with certain types of paranormal phenomenon – and capable of using many of them in our everyday lives.

Words, such as 'psychic' and 'paranormal' are widely used and cover a whole range of phenomena observable in the human and animal kingdoms. As research into these areas continues apace, new terms and definitions are being applied that try to nail down a specific phenomenon as distinct from all others – for instance, researchers who study the ability of human consciousness to affect the physical world use the term 'micro psychokinesis', or 'micro PK', to describe what they are looking for (see Chapter 5). However, this ability is closely related to a host of others – the ability to bend metal or move objects without touching them, for example, and even the ability to heal damage to the human body caused by injury or disease (see Chapter 6). Some of the theories about what energies might be at work are discussed in later chapters, but until we know whether we are dealing with many different manifestations of a single 'paranormal phenomenon', or many different phenomena (and such certainty can only come about after a prolonged period of research and verification), we have to be satisfied with some rather vague terms to describe them.

The phenomena explored in this book are at the very frontiers of science – and this at a time when orthodox science has been shaken to its foundations by new discoveries about the nature of the universe that have been made by quantum physicists still working through the implications of observations made by Einstein over seventy years ago. At the heart of this revolution is the crucial insight that all things – from the tiniest particle to the universe itself – are defined as much by their relationship with the environment around them as by their innate characteristics, and that if we try to understand the world simply by looking at its constituent parts, we will miss a crucial element in the equation. This is a holistic view of the world, a view that says that the whole really *is* more than the sum of its parts, and that you cannot describe a living system simply by describing all the little bits that make it up.

It may be no accident that this word 'holistic' is being

used to describe a new approach not just to abstract physics, but to many other fields of human activity. Orthodox medicine is increasingly turning to the holistic methods of acupuncture, homoeopathy, herbalism, and other treatments that aim to cure by taking the whole body into account, not just the affected or injured area. Modern business theory now stresses the importance of *systems* in which staff interact and communicate with each other so that they are fully aware of the part each person plays in the whole – no more compartmentalized departments with the right hand not knowing what the left hand is up to. And on the environmental front, we in the West have come to realize that our habits and lifestyle have a deep and lasting effect not just on our immediate environment, but on the planet as a whole.

As we approach the end of the millennium, it may be that we are beginning to think about our world in a new way. With our new perceptions of the world as a place full of interconnections and relationships – in which, to use the metaphor more commonly associated with chaos theory, a butterfly flapping its wings in the rainforests of the Amazon can be felt as a gust of wind in a London street – new forms of energy will be identified, explored and harnessed to our needs. Many of those forms of energy are to be found right here in these pages. I have long believed that the powers of the human mind are underused, and I hope that in the years ahead we will develop them further, and amaze ourselves with our own paranormal abilities.

Paul McKenna
London, March 1997

1 Ghosts

One in four people believes in ghosts and Britain is known as the ghost capital of the world. The Tower of London apparently has no less than thirty ghosts, including Edward V, Anne Boleyn, Sir Walter Raleigh and Guy Fawkes.

Ghosts, apparitions and hauntings are the most familiar and yet perhaps the least well understood of all paranormal phenomena. Ever since the early days of film, the restless spirits of the dead have been a staple diet for cinema audiences, from the eerie murmurs and laughter in *The Turn of the Screw* to the gory spectres on display in Hammer House of Horror movies and the spine-tingling terrors of *Poltergeist*. The literary ghost stretches even further back in time, with the apparition of the murdered Banquo in Shakespeare's *Macbeth* one of the earliest and most gruesome examples. In the nineteenth century, such writers as Charles Dickens and Edgar Allan Poe helped to encourage a taste for tales of supernatural spirits and phantoms that continues to this day.

Behind all this fiction lies the fact that the belief of having 'seen a ghost' is a very common occurrence indeed, and one that has been reported consistently since the earliest times. A series of polls carried out in the late nineteenth century by members of the London-based Society for Psychical Research (of which

Sigmund Freud and Aldous Huxley, among many others, were members) revealed that some 10 per cent of the population of Great Britain reported having seen a ghost, with that figure rising to 12 per cent when the census was extended to France, Germany and the United States. Even more astonishing are the results from surveys carried out in the 1980s by the National Opinion Research Council based in Chicago: this time, in an age when to admit to a paranormal experience would no longer have been considered quite so unorthodox, 42 per cent of the adult population of the USA, including an astonishing two-thirds of all widows, reported having had experience of ghostly phenomena. Very few of these people would claim to be psychically gifted or to have a special rapport with the spirits of the dead, and it is hard not to conclude that there is something going on.

Certainly there is no shortage of well-known people who have come forward and told of their own encounters with the dead. The actor Roger Moore, for instance, reports how he became 'rigid with fright' when a 'misty substance' came into the hotel room in which he was staying and floated across his bed. When the same thing happened the following night, Moore told the chambermaid about it. That evening, when he was getting ready for bed, Moore noticed a Bible open at Psalm 23 beside his bed. Special Agent 007 was not bothered again.

The actress Kim Novak vividly remembers her stay at the seventeenth-century Kentish mansion Chilham Castle during the filming of *The Amorous Adventures of Moll Flanders*. She went to her room one evening and put one of her favourite records on the record-player. 'I suddenly felt rather cold,' she recalls. 'A powerful force seemed to grab me round the waist. I was lifted off my feet and hurled against the wall.'

The supernatural experience of another actor, Telly Savalas, is especially remarkable because it was corroborated by a third party. He was driving one night through the countryside on Long Island, New York, when he ran out of petrol. He walked back down the road to a diner he had passed shortly before and asked for the nearest petrol station. Head towards the freeway, he was told. He had been walking for only a few minutes when he heard a voice asking whether he wanted a lift. He turned to see a man talking to him through the open window of a black Cadillac sedan, which had pulled up alongside him. Savalas got into the car, and the man drove him to the petrol station – he even lent the young actor a dollar to pay for his petrol. Savalas insisted that the man give him his name, address and phone number so that he could pay him back, and the man wrote this down on a piece of paper: Harry Agannis was the name. Shortly afterwards, Savalas dialled the number. A woman answered. She said that yes, Harry Agannis was her husband – but he had been dead for two years. Baffled, Savalas went round to her house and showed her the piece of paper. Mrs Agannis easily identified the handwriting as her husband's, and when Savalas described the clothes the man who had given him a lift had been wearing, she told him that these were the clothes her husband had been buried in.

There are many who will make strenuous efforts to deny the existence of ghosts and ridicule those who claim to have seen them. For me, the number and constancy of reported sightings is sufficient evidence that something paranormal is going on, and a far more interesting question is to ask, What exactly is a ghost? As with so many areas of paranormal and psychic research, definitions are hard to come by, and the distinction between ghosts and other paranormal phenomena is easily blurred. People can and frequently do experience apparitions of the living, but the term ghosts is usually reserved for manifestations of the dead. It is also reasonable to say that ghosts are associated in some way with someone who was once known to have been alive on earth – it makes no sense to talk of the ghosts of fictional characters.

Beyond this, distinctions are less clear-cut. For instance, if contact is being made with the spirits of the dead via a medium, or if a spirit appears to communicate with people conducting a séance, is it true to say that a ghost has appeared? Or is it more accurate to say that messages are being sent to and received from a spiritual plane of existence, so that rather than a ghost appearing in our world, we are intruding into theirs? By the same token, many people who have received advance warning of impending death or disaster feel that the warning has come from a spirit that is watching over them, a kind of guardian angel, perhaps associated with a loved one who has died. In this case, is it right to say that the warning has come from a ghost, or is a totally different kind of precognition at work – one cloaked in ghostly trappings because of the expectation of the 'percipient', the term paranormal researchers use, that such a warning must have come from beyond the grave, rather than in some even less explicable way?

One form of contact with otherworldly spirits that has been more and more widely observed is the phenomenon known as 'channelling'. Typically, a channeller will go into a 'trance', either spontaneous or induced, and become the medium by which a spirit communicates with the present day. The extent to which the channeller is 'taken over' varies considerably: often, words, ideas and images are the only medium used; sometimes, the channeller's personality is apparently displaced by that of the spirit, and observers note that the channeller uses a different voice and mannerisms, and perhaps speaks in a different language as well; more rarely, the mediated spirit appears to take over the being of the channeller entirely, using it to perform actions and display skills that are quite foreign to the channeller, and of which he or she may be totally unaware.

Examples of this are the award-winning English concert pianist John Lill, who maintains that he acts as a channel for Beethoven; and Luis Antonio Gasparetto, a Brazilian who believes he can act as a channel for several famous artists. In a live demonstration for Brazilian TV, Gasparetto painted for Rembrandt with his feet, Monet with his left hand, and Picasso with his right, completing three drawings simultaneously in twelve minutes flat. Such a feat may be possible given years of practice, but Gasparetto carries out the demonstration with such ease that it makes fascinating reading.

Perhaps the best known of all channellers was Jane Roberts, who for twenty years claimed to have channelled for a spirit who liked to be known as Seth. During channelling sessions, Seth would apparently take over Jane Roberts's body to the extent that she spoke with his voice. At one séance, it's claimed, the features of her face also changed shape when viewed in a mirror; at another one of her hands took on the appearance of a man's. When he first appeared, Seth said he was the spirit of Frank Withers, an English teacher from Elmira in California (local records confirmed the existence of this man), but he later described himself as 'an energy personality essence', and stated that parts of his essence had been reincarnated in many different people through the ages, including a caveman, a 'minor Pope' in the fourth century, a victim of the Spanish Inquisition, a Danish spice merchant, and a humble wife. As the spice merchant in seventeenth-century Denmark, he had known both Roberts and her husband – and this was his last full incarnation. The philosophy Seth expounded was complex and challenging, but his avowed intention was to communicate the simple truth that humanity is in charge of its own destiny, and can create its own reality by the nature of its thoughts, beliefs and actions. Jane Roberts was also a poet, and said that much of her work was inspired or written by Seth. During sessions, Roberts's husband took shorthand notes of all that Seth said, which were subsequently published in three volumes and remain the most comprehensive and compelling account we have of the extraordinary relationship between a spirit and a channeller. Jane Roberts never sought to channel for Seth before large paying audiences, as others who followed her and also claimed contact with Seth would do. She died in 1984 at the age of fifty-five.

Most experiences of channelling are positive and rewarding, but if the channelled spirit is malevolent and the channeller an unwilling agent, then the phenomenon is usually called 'possession' – a distressing and traumatic experience that is often treated in religious terms as a manifestation of evil. Indeed, channelling is frequently associated with religious experience, especially at the evangelical-charismatic end of the belief spectrum. Many channellers feel that they are communicating on behalf of religious figures – saints, prophets, holy men, sometimes even Jesus Christ himself – or for angels, or for deities themselves. Looking back to the days of early civilizations in China, Egypt, Persia, Greece and some Celtic lands, we find that priests and other religious figures devoted a great deal of time and energy to channelling for their respective gods. Indeed, this phenomenon has long been a central belief of the Judaeo-Christian tradition, since the Old Testament prophets effectively acted as mouthpieces for God. Thus, every Sunday in any church where the Nicene Creed is said, people effectively assert their belief in channelling with the words: 'He it was who spoke through the Prophets.'

Returning specifically to ghosts and apparitions, theories as to exactly what we are witnessing are many and varied. For some, they are mental hallucinations communicated telepathically to the percipient, but this cannot explain why, when many different people witness an apparition simultaneously, the details they remember – though seldom contradictory – will often vary significantly. Others consider them to be manifestations of a subliminal consciousness, beyond time and space, in which both the living and the dead can share, but this seems to belie the fact that so many ghosts are distinctly associated with a *particular* place and a *particular* person. Still others regard them as more or less meaningless fragments of energy left behind in the 'psychic ether'; or as imprints or vibrations projected into an object or locality, and which are visible to the receptive or to anyone with a specific relationship with the source, and to others when disturbed. A simpler explanation is that ghosts are genuine manifestations of the human spirit, which has survived its corporeal form; some go further and believe that the spirit has become trapped in the plane of material existence and cannot reach its own plane for any of a number of possible reasons – unfinished business such as revenge, for instance, or plain unwillingness to leave occasioned, perhaps, by a violent or sudden death in especially tragic circum- stances, or deep love for someone who is still alive (a reason often given when channelled spirits are asked why they wish to communicate with the living).

It is currently believed by some that while ghosts do have an 'objective reality' and are not just figments of overactive imaginations, they nevertheless need to exploit the psychic energies of the living before they can make their presence felt – and that therefore their ability to appear is dependent on them being observed. This theory ties in with discoveries about the 'quantum universe', which suggest that the distinction between subjective and objective reality is in any case a false one, because nothing can be entirely one or the other, but everything is an amalgam of the two.

This way of looking at ghosts is, however, challenged by a remarkable piece of footage taken by a security camera at the Butterfly nightclub in Oldham in 1991. It was viewed after a disturbance was reported at the club in the early hours of the morning, long after closing time. The alarm had gone off and the police were already at the scene. Yet there was absolutely no sign of a break-in. When they looked at the video evidence, they claim they saw a man in short-sleeved shirt and dark trousers walk down a corridor and then straight into the room where the cash was kept, even though the door was closed and locked – as could clearly be seen on the tape. It seemed that the phantom thief had simply walked through the door. Many people have argued that the video is a fake. However, the footage of the intruder is timed at precisely the moment the alarm went off, and for insurance reasons the tapes were logged and loaded very carefully, so there was no real possibility of a mix-up.

Such theories and events give us plenty of food for thought, if no very solid conclusions. The general lack of definitions and the possibility of confusing one type of paranormal experience with another combine to make ghostly experiences very difficult to research with any kind of accuracy; and the problem is exacerbated by the fact that hauntings tend to occur at the instigation of the ghost, not of the people who believe they have seen them. However, there are fortunately some places which appear to be haunted with great regularity and sometimes by a large number of different spirits; and there are also people who seem to have the ability to see the spirits of the dead at will, even if these spirits do not seem to be specifically appearing to them. In addition, some people, it appears, have developed a particular expertise at identifying ghosts – often using techniques to measure temperature changes in the air around them, and their effect on magnetic fields. What we do know about the subject is largely derived from such people and places. In the following pages, I will describe the activities of just two, the 'ghost-hunter' Eddie Burks, and the channeller and psychic Rosemary Altea.

Like many people who claim to have psychic gifts, Rosemary Altea had an unhappy childhood. One of four sisters in the family, she was singled out by both her parents – felt unloved and unwanted, blamed for every mishap, beaten without mercy and starved of all affection. There was a belief in the family that Rosemary might turn out like her grandmother Eliza, who heard voices and, believing she was mad, admitted herself to a mental hospital. Rosemary also was prone to 'seeing things' – hearing voices and seeing faces that weren't really there – and often her mother would shout at her that she'd end up 'in the Towers', the mental hospital in the Alteas' home town of Leicester.

The things she saw and the strange sensations that sometimes engulfed her terrified the young girl, and yet there was no one for her to talk to about these strange visions, and she too began to believe that she must be destined for insanity. Of all the unnerving sensations Rosemary Altea suffered, there was one which would come back again and again: it was the feeling that her face was being peeled away, as if it were no more than a rubber mask. She learned to dread this feeling more than any other.

It was not until she was in her early thirties, married and with a daughter of her own, that Rosemary began to understand something about her strange visions.

They were entertaining her husband's boss, Terry Maxwell, one night for dinner, and he began to talk about an encounter with a spiritualist who had picked him out from an audience and then revealed intimate details about his life, things no one who was not close to him could possibly have known about. He then asked Rosemary whether she thought someone might be guarding over her three-year-old daughter. Her tentative reply was that yes, she felt somehow that her husband's grandfather might be watching over her daughter.

Terry Maxwell excitedly asked her husband for his grandfather's ring, then placed it between two halves of a pack of cards and asked Rosemary to choose between them: if she picked a king or a knave, then it would be a man – perhaps her husband's grandfather – who was watching over her daughter; if she picked a queen, it would be a woman. As she concentrated on the ring, Rosemary felt the familiar and dreadful sensation creeping over her: her face being tugged aside, pulled away from her. Her face went white and she said she felt a powerful force take control of her body, paralysing her, pushing her down into the sofa as if beneath a crushing weight. Her husband watched aghast, and ran over to help her. The atmosphere in the room had become very cold. Then, as quickly as it had stolen over her, the sensation disappeared. She brought her hands up to her face, as if to verify that it was still there, weeping and trembling with fear.

In the aftermath of this incident, Rosemary claims she began to see apparitions with increasing regularity: she claims they would suddenly appear in a chair opposite, or she would wake in the middle of the night to find 'ghosts' in her bedroom. She realized that she had always been haunted by these terrifying apparitions, which seemed to be taking an increasingly dominant part in her life. Fearful that she would be certified insane, she told no one and suffered the 'hauntings' in isolation. The feeling of her face being peeled away recurred. As the intensity of the experiences increased, she began to feel that she was being transported to a different world, in the company of strangers whose substance was different to her own. Throughout this difficult period, only her strong and sincere faith in God stood between her and despair.

Then, by chance, she encountered a spiritualist healer by the name of Paul Denham, who believed that Rosemary Altea had the gift of mediumship, and was capable of developing truly exceptional psychic powers. And, though a long and difficult road lay ahead of her, Paul and his wife, Irene Denham, believed that the faces and bodies and voices which had troubled her for as long as she could remember were not manifestations of madness in her, but of a very different kind: they were manifestations of a spirit world that exists in another set of dimensions from our own.

Under Paul Denham's gentle tutelage, Rosemary Altea gradually lost her fear of the unknown world that had intertwined itself so deeply with hers. One night as she went to bed after a session with Paul in which she had, for the first time, been able to welcome the communion with the spirit world without the customary dread, she asked for God's guidance, praying for a sign that she was on the right track. Almost immediately, she claims, she heard voices . . .

singing . . . She recognized the song as Psalm 23 – 'The Lord's my shepherd'. Sitting up in bed, she looked around her but could see nothing, only hear a sweet, ethereal chorus. She realized after a while that she was listening to angels singing.

Rosemary became increasingly comfortable with her 'psychic' encounters; yet there was still one element of her life that seemed dark and frightening: that irresistible force that she says she felt sometimes took control of her body and made her feel as if a mask were being pulled off her face. The suggestion was made to her that this might be a powerful spirit guide, who would one day reveal himself to her. Rosemary didn't think much of the idea at the time, but there was something very special about the man who told her this: he seemed to understand her, to feel as she did. He had his own spirit guide, an American Indian chief named Red Feather. While he and Rosemary were talking, he interrupted to say that there was a figure standing behind her. He said the man's name was William Edward. He was dressed in a sergeant's uniform. He was a proud man, intolerant of imperfection. As he went on talking about the man before him, Rosemary listened in fascination. Here was an almost total stranger describing in the clearest possible detail the appearance and character of her own father, William Edwards.

Many things clicked into place for Rosemary that night: maybe there really was life after death; maybe she and others like her were able to make contact with that life and the world it inhabited; and it might be possible to derive knowledge of that world through a spirit guide – someone who watches over the world we know – just as this man said.

She says her own spirit guide made his appearance to her not long afterwards. He is Grey Eagle, an Apache Indian, a proud, strong and commanding man, and a highly developed being in the spirit world. Guided by his powerful, reassuring presence, Rosemary began to work as a medium, initially giving private consultations, then appearing in public to help people make contact with loved ones who had departed, bringing comfort and hope to the bereaved. And as well as helping people in the living world, Grey Eagle would bring her people from the spirit world who she says were suffering terrible torments, unable to continue their journey through the life of the spirit, perhaps because of the awful circumstances surrounding their death.

Rosemary Altea's fascinating autobiography, *The Eagle and the Rose*, describes some of the many people she has worked with over the years, and there are a number of common themes. The first and most obvious is the great persistence and strength those apparently in the spirit world show in their desire to contact those they have left behind. In some cases, she claims, they have even appeared to her *before* the sitting itself, when she knows nothing about who her client will be or the circumstances and events which have led them to consult her. She also claims that communication with those in the spirit world is very much a two-way process – it does not simply consist of words drifting mysteriously out of the ether, words which may or may not have relevance to those living in the material world. There is a sense in which the desire to find a medium through which to open a channel of communication between the two worlds is driven not by the bereaved but by those who have moved on to the spirit world. They seem to have a strong desire to tell those they have left behind that a part of them – and perhaps the most important part – has actually survived death, and that they can continue to watch over and provide guidance for their loved ones from the spiritual plane.

Rosemary Altea certainly believes she sees people from the spirit world all the time and wherever she goes, whether out shopping, or on holiday, or in her own bedroom at home – so much so that you would think that she would become irritated by them, though her faith in God and the unshakeable foundations of her relationship with Grey Eagle seem to keep her remarkably gentle and tolerant.

Rosemary Altea is clearly a fascinating woman – all the more so when you consider the miserable circumstances in which the early part of her life took place. But of all the many fascinating aspects of her story, the one that intrigues me most is her firm assertion that the motive force behind her work is to help people in the spirit world, rather than people in our world – although of course her work with the sick and bereaved is much more than just a welcome side-effect. What this suggests is that there may be a reason behind every ghost story – a reason we may not understand, but which is there for us to discover if we can develop the means to do so.

If the world of Rosemary Altea is strange, perhaps even incredible, to many, the work of Eddie Burks, though equally hard to explain, takes place on more familiar territory. His business is investigating ghosts and hauntings, and he has been called to many places around Britain to help bring peace, it's claimed, to restless spirits. He is probably best known for his work at Coutt's Bank in the Strand. Staff at the prestigious bank believed they were being plagued by a headless ghost, often not in the best of tempers, and were so terrified that many of them threatened to leave unless something was done. Eddie Burks was called in and he claims that he immediately encountered the ghost, who complained that he had been unjustly beheaded. He seemed impatient, and irritated that he had had to wait for so long before someone came to help him. After a brief conversation, Eddie was apparently able to send the spirit on his way in peace. The ghost was later identified as Thomas Howard, Fourth Duke of Norfolk, who had been beheaded on the orders of Queen Elizabeth I in 1572 for supposedly taking part in a plot to overthrow her.

It was this incident that brought Eddie Burks to the attention of the public, but he had been working as a psychic for many years. As with Rosemary Altea, familiarity and contact with the spirit world is what he believes gives him abilities as a healer, and he had been working in this capacity since 1975. Eight years later, while visiting the College of Psychic Studies in London, he encountered a 'trapped soul' – a man who had suffered from a mild deformity in his lifetime and had lived a life of drudgery, in servitude to a bullying master. His memories of his miserable life had such a powerful grip on his emotions that he was unable to let them go, and ever since his death he had lingered near his old haunts, unable to move forward. Eddie Burks managed to release him, and has done the same service for many other ghosts and apparitions.

Eddie defines a ghost as 'an earthbound spirit', one who is unable to make the transition to the spirit world. The reason for the earthly entrapment of many of Eddie Burks's ghostly clients is that they have apparently departed life in violent or traumatic circumstances, and it is not unusual for him to take a hand in easing the suffering associated with tragedies that make headline news. On the night of 19 August 1989 the Thames riverboat the *Marchioness* was sunk after a collision with a dredger and more than sixty people lost their lives. Shortly afterwards, Eddie Burks was approached by a young woman who claimed she was disturbed by the feeling that some unknown spirit had begun to haunt her. When she visited him, according to Burks, a spirit immediately presented itself. At first Eddie thought she was a victim of the Lockerbie bombing; but then the spirit, whom he identified as a woman of nineteen or twenty, explained that she had drowned on the *Marchioness*. Apparently, through Eddie, she was able to relive the dreadful, panic-stricken ordeal of her death and find release.

The ghosts Eddie Burks has encountered seem to attach themselves to people who offer them some hope of gaining their freedom from the material world – for the haunted person, this may be a frightening experience, especially if the spirit is very angry and bitter about his or her life on earth. The key to unlocking their shackles, it's claimed, is to project feelings of love towards them, but this may be hard to do, especially if the haunted person is very frightened.

One young couple moved into a brand-new house, but the wife always felt badly about the place. The first night she slept there she woke in the night, feeling as if she was being suffocated by a heavy weight pressing down on her body. Over the coming months they noticed cold patches in the house that it seemed impossible to heat up. The wife, Joanne, felt as if she were being watched.

A year later Joanne had separated from her husband and lived alone with her young son. One night she says she felt a hand on her shoulder, then all the light bulbs in the hallway went out and she thought she heard the sound of someone running downstairs. She searched the house from top to bottom for the intruder but could find no one. Going out into the hall, she saw her son Nick standing at the top of the stairs. Seconds later he was tumbling down, as if pushed by an unseen hand, and lay bruised and crying at her feet.

Joanne decided she had had enough. She asked the local Catholic church to perform an exorcism, and for a while things were calmer. Then she believes she saw the ghost of a man in her living room. Shortly afterwards she was put in touch with Eddie Burks, who came to her house and claims he encountered a very angry, turbulent spirit. He had lived in the thirteenth century, and had been treated as an outcast because of his strange manner, then branded a witch and drowned by being bound to a log and thrown in a river. Many times in his life he had been stoned or beaten, and his only friends were the stray dogs that came to share his food. Sometimes, in order to fend off the attacks of the local villagers, he would pretend to have the supernatural powers they accused him of using. His wretched existence and unjust death had apparently left him earthbound for many centuries. Now he had attached himself to Joanne in the hope that she could help him escape the thrall of his terrible memories and destructive emotions.

Eddie believes he was able to help bring him the love he had missed in his life, and perhaps did not know how to find, and witnessed his step away from the earth and towards the spirit world in the company of two friars. But this was not the end for Joanne, and Eddie was to visit her many more times and help what she believed were ghosts who had come to haunt her.

Not all ghost stories concern tragedy, however.

Sheila and Larry Duggan lived in Essex with their four children. On New Year's Day 1993, many parents' worst nightmare came true: a fire started in the house and spread rapidly through every room until the house was engulfed. Despite the danger from smoke and flames, the Duggans managed to get out with three of their children. But the fourth, eight-year-old Michelle, was trapped upstairs. There was no way back into the house, and from their garden the family watched in horror as they saw Michelle's little fists beating against the windowpane and heard her cries above the cruel roar of the fire. She was too small to reach the window, and it seemed only a matter of time before she was overcome by smoke. Then an extraordinary thing happened. There was the noise of smashing glass, and an ornament came flying through the window. Moments later Michelle herself came hurtling through the hole in the glass and landed on the tarmac five metres below.

Michelle was totally unhurt, despite the fall. The hole in the window through which she had come was apparently far too small for her to have passed through, and there was no way she could have climbed up to the window: firemen who were first into the house after the fire has been doused reported that no chair or other piece of furniture had been dragged over to the window, so how could Michelle possibly have climbed up to it? Only Michelle herself was quite clear what had happened: she says her great-grandfather, who had died some years earlier, had appeared in the room beside her, broken the glass, and pushed her through to safety.

With that heartening story, we will have to leave the world of ghosts and spirits. Thinking about Rosemary Altea and Eddie Burks, they seem to be at opposite ends of the spectrum in many respects, and yet there are two key qualities that unite them. The first is their very firm belief that their role is not to free people of a wretched ghost who is ruining their lives or their business, but rather to help liberate those spirits which, for whatever reason, have apparently been unable to escape the shackles of material existence. It is common for us to see ghosts as rather a curse, but neither Eddie nor Rosemary see them this way at all – they see them as they would see anyone who is evidently suffering and in need of help. By contrast, the 'ghostbuster' approach to the spirit world – the idea that ghosts have to be driven out and banished for ever – seems churlish, and even irresponsible.

The second common thread is that both these people believe very strongly in the transcendent power of love, and hold it central to their philosophy and their understanding of the spirit world. It is as if this powerful, enriching emotion, which can bind two people together for a lifetime, may also be a reflection or manifestation of a power far greater than we could imagine – a power that binds the universe together and which, if we make an effort to explore it more fully, may provide the key to many experiences that we currently describe as paranormal.

One of the themes of this book will be that there is no absolute dividing line between experiences and events we call normal and those we think of as paranormal. Rather, all such happenings are on a continuum, with ordinary observable things such as walking down a street or talking to a friend at one end, and extraordinary and rare experiences such as 'seeing a ghost' or communicating with the 'spirit' of someone who has died at the other. Between is a grey area, ambiguous and enigmatic. For instance, consider the statistic quoted earlier – that two-thirds of all widows in the USA reported having seen a ghost. Now in some respects this may seem remarkable – so many paranormal experiences, so many ghosts! Yet in other ways this is the most ordinary and predictable statistic. It is often observed that people who have been together for many years develop a kind of affinity that enables them to communicate in ways not easily explained. They will share thoughts without vocalizing them, predict each other's needs (even when these are not of the routine kind), and be aware of each other's presence or arrival without any obvious sensory means. It is almost as if the two have created a field in which they both share, or, to use Seth's words, their 'energy personality essences' have developed the ability to communicate at a non-physical level of existence.

Given that this kind of readily observed communication is not dependent on any physical senses or capabilities – speech, hearing, sight – is it possible that it survives the decease of the physical body? Certainly if it does, this would explain why widows and widowers continue to 'feel the presence' of their loved ones and often enjoy their company after they have died.

Perhaps, over the course of many years together, human couples create the reality of a relationship that exists not just at the physical level of life on earth, but at a spiritual level that is not affected by death and possibly enables communication beyond the grave.

Could it be that, in the case of Rosemary Altea, for instance, she is genuinely in contact with the spirits of the departed, but the forms that the resulting communication take are conditioned by her own deep belief in the importance of human love? This would perhaps be the least surprising conclusion we could draw in this chapter. Who says that life has to divide up neatly into separate bits and pieces called 'ghosts' and 'spirits' and 'channellers' that we can assemble into a simple and predictable paranormal event? Even assuming that we fully understand each individual item, we know from experience that combinations are always unpredictable, that if you combine two separate and different things, the result is frequently more than the sum of those two things – more than the 'predictable result'. This is especially true of living things, for both the source of life and its infinite variety appear to be closely associated with dualisms and combinations: man and woman; form and content; space and time; body and spirit; mind and matter; science and faith. Viewed in this light, you would expect Rosemary and a 'spirit' to interact very differently from, say, Jane Roberts and that same spirit. In each case, you would expect to witness a different paranormal event. This apparent lack of consistency – of recurrence – always seems to give ammunition to the sceptics. How come this 'spirit' says one thing through this channeller and another thing through that one? Perhaps we should welcome such inconsistencies. Maybe the rationalist approach has resulted in some scientists concentrating too hard on the parts, and so missing the event itself.

2 UFOs

Fifteen million people worldwide, including two former US presidents, claim to have seen an unidentified flying object. According to Dr Richard Haines, 15 per cent of all commercial and military pilots will have some kind of UFO contact during their career.

Are we being visited from outer space?

This question tends to divide people more absolutely than any of the many controversial issues raised in this book. Those who believe they have seen an Unidentified Flying Object (UFO) are not in any doubt that what they witnessed was not an atmospheric effect, nor an astronomical phenomenon such as a meteor or shooting star, nor a familiar and mundane object such as an aeroplane or helicopter. Those who deride their claims are equally certain that such people are either gullible or predisposed to look for other-than-rational explanations for anything that seems remotely out of the ordinary – or probably both.

One thing we do know is that military authorities in virtually every nation in the world with the money, equipment and resources to do so take UFOs very seriously indeed. And in two notable cases, top military personnel have actually admitted in public to having dealt with cases they consider to be genuine. This is unusual: there are many cases of retired military officers discussing their UFO experiences, but when it comes to those whose careers are still active, secrecy is usually the name of the game. One can only assume that in these cases the evidence was simply too overwhelming to be concealed.

The first is one of the most well-documented series of UFO sightings of all time, with eyewitness evidence accumulated from over 2,500 witnesses – including members of the armed forces and police officers. The events took place in Belgium over the winter of 1989–90, with the most dramatic sighting occurring on 30 March. The incident began with a number of radar units locating a UFO. At this stage, 'UFO' would have meant exactly that – radar is not a very precise tool, and it is seldom that accurate identification can be made without further information. So it was routine procedure to send in a pair of F16 fighters to investigate. They succeeded in finding the target, but as the planes circled and the pilots got in close enough to use their own eyes they could hardly believe what they saw.

It was moving very slowly, as slowly as twenty-five miles per hour, yet managing to maintain an altitude of around 2,000 metres. It was an awesome size and flat – not saucer-shaped, because it was shaped like a diamond with one point clipped off, but lacking any vertical lines. Lights winked around its edges as it hung effortlessly in the air and the fighter planes, tiny by comparison, buzzed around it.

Then, without warning, it accelerated to a phenomenal speed, leaving the powerful fighters circling empty space, and dropped down to around 200 metres. This manoeuvre seemed to take no more than a second. The F16s followed, but it was some time before they located the UFO again. Once again it had taken up its stately position at 2,000 metres and was hanging gracefully in the air. As soon as the F16s closed in, however, it dropped out of the skies like a stone again, and the planes were unable to follow fast enough to keep track. Twice more this happened, and twice more the fighters were left stranded as the enormous craft executed its simple but totally effective evasive manoeuvre.

Belgian Air Force chief Colonel Wilfried de Brouwer was impressed when his pilots reported the incident. The particular evasive manoeuvre described was not just beyond the capabilities of any known aircraft, it also seemed to imply a foreknowledge of what aerial tactics might be used to shake off a terrestrial fighter plane, and also of the fact that radar would be unable to track an object flying below 200 metres altitude. It all suggested an intelligent guiding hand at the helm. De Brouwer ruled out the idea that what his pilots had seen might have been caused by freak atmospheric phenomena. (Indeed, any air-defence system unable to distinguish between the vagaries of the weather and a vast flying object would be of dubious value.) De Brouwer stood by his pilots, who were convinced that they had witnessed something extraordinary that night. Later, the flight recorders from the two F16s were made available, and the evidence of the sophisticated equipment locking on to and then losing track of the UFO is indisputable. And given that the F16 is the most advanced jet fighter in the world, what kind of aircraft could possibly have evaded the two planes so effortlessly?

This was the best documented of a whole series of sightings over this period. But they began not in Belgium but the former USSR. The evidence for the following sighting comes from a report in the Soviet newspaper *The Workers' Tribune*, which was based on the written testimony of Lieutenant-Colonel A. Semyenchenko, a pilot in the Soviet Air Force. After receiving his orders to take off on a routine patrol, Semyenchenko was astonished to encounter a vast, disc-shaped object in the skies about eighty-five miles north-east of Moscow:

I made visual contact with the target, distinguished by two blinking white lights, at 2205 hours . . . it was ahead and to the right, at an angle of 10 degrees. The target changed altitude by up to 1,000 metres, and also altered direction of flight. With the permission of the command centre, I locked on to the heat source, after checking to ensure that my armaments were disengaged.

The target did not respond to the 'Identity: friend or foe?' request. As well as the target, three or four regular scheduled airliners could be observed on the [radar] screen. As instructed by the command centre, I carried out a banked turn. While completing the turn, I observed a luminescent phenomenon, reminiscent of the aurora borealis but less bright, to the north and north-west.

I approached the target to within about 500 or 600 metres. I passed above the target, trying to discern its precise nature. I observed only two bright white flashing lights. I briefly saw the target silhouetted against the illuminated city [of Pereslavel Zalesky].

Flights of fancy are not encouraged among military personnel, yet here was an experienced pilot reporting observation of an alien in an area within which he would have patrolled many times before, and whose characteristics he could have been expected to know as well as you or I know the layout of the street where we live. The reference to the aurora borealis, the Northern Lights, suggests that he is perfectly familiar with the atmospheric phenomena which some believe account for many UFO sightings, and which can certainly play tricks on the inexperienced.

Semyenchenko was not the only person whose account of these events reached the desk of General Igor Malzev, Chief of the General Staff of Soviet Air Forces, in the days following the event: as he admitted in the same newspaper article, more than a hundred statements describing the UFO had been recorded. Among them was the testimony of a Captain V. Birin:

> The object was like a flying saucer with two very bright lights at the edges. Its diameter was approximately 100–200 metres (judging by the shining lights) . . . The momentum was determined by the two bright lights: the more frequently they flashed, the faster the speed of the UFO, and vice versa. While hovering, the vessel's lights were very dim . . .

According to Malzev, this feature had been noticed by all those who witnessed the flight of the UFO. He also confirmed that the object had been observed by several nearby radar centres, and gave further details gleaned from the mass of evidence:

When the object flew horizontally, the line of the lights was parallel to the horizon. During vertical movement it rotated and was perpendicular to the ground. In addition, the object was able to rotate around its axis and perform an S-turn, while flying either horizontally or at right angles to the ground . . . The UFO flew at a speed exceeding that of a modern jet fighter by two or three times.

It was not only the velocity of the object that was astonishing:

The motion of the UFO was not accompanied by any kind of sound, and was notable for its remarkable manoeuvrability . . . It appeared that the UFO was completely devoid of inertia. Or to put it another way, they had somehow 'come to terms' with gravity.

The gracefulness, manoeuvrability and speed of the craft were qualities the Belgians had noticed too. Was this the same spaceship? Or a sister ship from the same alien armada? Whatever the answer, it seems impossible to dismiss the eyewitness accounts of so many people, especially when some, like military pilots, are experienced in observation and unlikely to be easily hoodwinked.

Reports such as these lend credibility to the idea that UFOs may occasionally be manned craft visiting our planet from outer space. So too, in my view, does the blanket of official secrecy which is drawn over the whole subject in most countries, including our own. Staggering though it may seem, in the 1960s US civilian pilots could be given a ten-year prison sentence simply for passing on information about UFO sightings to the world at large. This attitude stemmed partly from the belief that people would become dangerously hysterical if they thought the nightmare scenario of many a 1950s B-movie was about to come true and the aliens had landed. As Orson Welles's famous broadcast of H. G. Wells's *The War of the Worlds* demonstrated, people felt this threat keenly, and perhaps the authorities were right to be wary of alarming people when, in all probability, they themselves may have been unsure what was going on. However, as the authorities soon came to discover, denying the very existence of UFOs was not enough to quell speculation. If they weren't from space, where were these strange craft from? At the height of the Cold War, the answer was obvious: Russia. There was a widespread belief in the military that many UFOs were in fact secret weapons developed by the USSR to spy on or attack America. From the point of view of the military leaders of the day, it must have been hard to know what was the less palatable option: declaring that aliens were reconnoitring the planet with intentions unknown, or admitting that the Soviet Union might have developed a secret weapon that could penetrate US air space at will.

Many researchers in this field believe that firm, physical evidence of extraterrestrial visitation has been in the hands of the US military authorities for many years. Perhaps the most significant evidence for this derived from the events that took place in the vicinity of Roswell, New Mexico, in July 1947.

The story begins with an apparently unremarkable UFO sighting – a bright, disc-shaped object sweeping low over the dramatic landscape of the south-western United States. Next day a farmer named William Brazel was out riding with his young son. On the outskirts of his land, they came across some strange debris – it looked like wreckage from something, but the farmer couldn't work out how it might piece together into something recognizable. There was something weird about the stuff, no doubt about that, and Brazel decided to inform the local sheriff, get him out to have a look.

If Brazel had been expecting a quiet chat with his friend the sheriff, he was sadly mistaken. After his call, the sheriff immediately contacted the local US Air Force base, and within hours a delegation from the 509th Bomb Group Intelligence Office was on the scene. They immediately set about clearing away every last scrap of debris, loading it in conditions of great secrecy aboard a B-29 bomber, and spiriting it away. A team of men then searched every inch of the surrounding area for more evidence: if they found any, they packed that up too. Soon an official version of the story was put out: the wreckage had been identified as coming from one of the Air Force's brand-new weather balloons.

Brazel, meanwhile, was taken into custody for a week. Nobody attempted to explain, least of all to Brazel himself, why catching sight of a few bits and pieces of a weather balloon and reporting it to the authorities should have been regarded as behaviour deserving a week under lock and key. Nor why all documentation and evidence regarding the crash wreckage should have been classified ever since. Nor why attempts by an elected member of the US Senate to view the debris were refused. It must have been some balloon . . .

The official story has been coming apart at the seams ever since it was released. Most decisively, the officer in charge of the operation to clean up and remove the wreckage, Major Jesse Marcel, has rubbished the weather-balloon explanation, and declared that some of the material he handled that day was 'like nothing on earth'. Among the items recovered was a piece of metal barely thicker than tin foil, which was so strong that it could not be dented with a full-size sledgehammer. Brazel confirms that some of the metal debris he saw was highly unusual – why else would he have contacted the authorities? Since then, researchers have contacted more than 150 eyewitnesses, who corroborate this account of the events at Roswell with a remarkable degree of unanimity.

More recently, it has become clear that this was not the only crash in the vicinity of Roswell. There was another in 1949. This time, it was not just debris that was recovered. According to sources close to the incident, six aliens were allegedly found, one of them still alive.

What were they like, these 'Extraterrestrial Biological Entities' (EBEs) as they were termed in the official jargon of the day? According to reports, they were three to four feet tall, with smooth, greyish skin, delicate humanoid features, and eyes rather like those of a cat. Still more remarkable, American documentary film-makers claim to have seen footage of military personnel in friendly communication with the surviving being. If this spool of 16-millimetre film really does exist, along with the bodies of the dead aliens, then it lies within the power of the authorities to confirm once and for all that alien beings really have visited our planet.

Further confirmation that strange events were taking place in the vicinity of Roswell at this time was provided in 1986, when the eminent physicist Professor Robert Saurbacher, who had been a top-level researcher for the US Department of Defense in the 1950s, declared to an astonished American public that the 1947 Roswell incident was only one of a number of recoveries of alien spacecraft. He described how he himself had handled some of the incredibly strong but lightweight metal, and averred that details of the UFO crashes were classified as the most secret information in the possession of the US Government, with the full details known only to a handful of members of the military/political inner sanctum. Saurbacher's testimony was efficiently rebutted by the authorities, and, had he been a lone voice, his story might not have been believed. Taken together with other evidence and eyewitness accounts of Roswell, in my view there is every reason to believe that he is telling the truth. We have been visited from outer space.

Known US military interest in UFOs seems to have dated from the Roswell period. Less than a year after Roswell, an incident took place at Goldman Air Base, Kentucky. At one in the afternoon, reports began to come in to the control room at the base that motorists had sighted a huge, glowing, saucer-shaped object. At first these reports were dismissed as fanciful, but then guards at nearby Fort Knox, where the US gold reserve is stored, rang in and confirmed that a UFO nearly a third of a mile across was gliding over the area.

Overimaginative motorists are one thing, but the world's largest deposit of gold is quite another: immediately, Mustang fighters were sent up to investigate. As soon as they approached, however, the flying saucer climbed rapidly to 6,600 metres and, displaying astonishing agility in the skies, disappeared behind a cloud. Simultaneously, Flight Leader Thomas Mantell – who had reported over his radio that he was tracking a 'silvery metal disc of tremendous size' – also disappeared. The rest of the Mustangs searched for a while, then returned to base. There was no sign of Mantell.

It was not long before the wreckage of his plane was discovered scattered over a wide area. What had happened? It looked like the result of a mid-air collision, but it takes two aircraft to collide: what happened to the other? Mantell was an experienced pilot who wouldn't have made an elementary mistake; nor did it seem at all likely that the Mustang had simply disintegrated. Mysteriously, the military claimed that his body had also been recovered, but wouldn't allow anyone, not even his immediate family, to see it.

Later in 1948, in North Dakota, an F51 fighter was coming in to land when it was buzzed by a UFO. The object in question was intensely bright and astonishingly agile. Since details of both this and the previous encounter had leaked out, inevitably the two incidents were associated, and public interest became feverish. The situation was worsened when the depth of military concern over the incidents became clear. A leaked memorandum from Strategic Air Command to the Air Technical Intelligence Center referred to 'interplanetary craft' and declared that the reports of UFO sightings from seasoned and reliable Air Force personnel were 'undoubtedly real'. (The full text of this report was destroyed in 1955.) Further documents confirm that military leaders at the time undoubtedly believed that piloted spacecraft were on the loose. For instance, the following passage occurs in a letter to USAF Commander Brigadier-General George Schlugen:

> It is the position of this command that the so-called flying disc phenomena are something real and not visionary . . . manoeuvrability and evasive action when contacted by human craft lend belief to the possibility that the objects are controlled.

It was as a direct result of UFO sightings in this period that official US policy regarding the phenomenon was formulated. An investigative body, classified as Grade A Secret and named 'Project Sign', was instructed to look into the loss of the Mustang. Its initial finding suggested that the giant saucer had been real enough – much to the irritation of the then USAF Chief of Staff, General Vandenberg, who promptly burnt the report. When Project Sign's findings were made public, all suggestions of interplanetary spaceships were dismissed and 'rational' explanations given instead. The project was formally closed.

Behind the scenes, however, Project Sign turned into Project Blue Book, which would continue to investigate UFO sightings for many years to come. From this time on, US policy seems to have been to take the 'alien threat' very seriously, but also to ensure that whatever they discovered was kept secret. Many documents describing UFO sightings have come to light thanks to freedom of information legislation in the

USA – but many more remain excluded from public scrutiny.

Despite that veil of secrecy, evidence about the nature of Project Blue Book *has* been slowly seeping out. The most startling and extraordinary information concerns an Air Force base located in the desert about eighty miles north-west of Las Vegas: usually referred to as 'Area 51', or 'Dreamland'.

Area 51 is the most secret place in the Western world. It was built in the 1950s, but the US Government and military have always strenuously denied that it even exists. However, satellite photos clearly show an extensive base with huge hangars and a network of runways. As far as it is discussed at all, Area 51 is known as an aircraft test facility – the Stealth bomber was created there. But a number of intelligence agents – who go by codenames such as 'Falcon' and 'Condor' – have said that Area 51 has another purpose. According to them, the incident at Roswell was only the first of many extraterrestrial visitations: over the years, many more alien life forms have landed in the same area, and they claim the US Government has been colluding with them.

One of the driving forces behind this sensational claim is John Lear, son of the man who designed the Lear jet. John Lear is the only man to hold every flying certificate issued by the Federal Aviation Authority, and has flown over 160 different types of aircraft around the world, including many missions for the CIA. His bizarre claims that a deal between the 'EBEs' and the US Government was struck between 1979 and 1981. In exchange for the right to share the alien technology – which is thought to include 'gravity drive systems' and 'force-field technology' – the US authorities purportedly agreed to turn a blind eye to the kind of experiments the EBEs wanted to carry out. These might necessitate both animal mutilations and human abductions, two kinds of incident which have now been repeatedly and insistently reported for many years. Needless to say, Lear has been widely vilified for his outrageous claims.

It is unfortunate that, with such heavy military involvement in this issue, many of the witnesses most likely to know the true story are unwilling to reveal their real names. It is sensible to be wary about people who prefer to remain anonymous, although various researchers claim to have uncovered the true identities of some. As the evidence of some kind of collusion mounts, it has become increasingly difficult to dismiss all those who have come forward as fantasists.

Mike Hunt, a former employee of the US Atomic Energy Commission, claims to have observed flying saucers while working at Area 51: he claims he was warned never to talk about anything he saw there; and he had the distinct impression that some activities at the base were not taking place under the authority of the Air Force.

Former USAF Lieutenant-Colonel Wendelle Stevens has co-written a book about UFO incidents since the Second World War, and reports the existence of a large test facility – involving perhaps 800–1,000 personnel – constructed at a Navy Auxiliary base. According to several informants the purpose of this facility – which was mostly built underground – was to research UFO propulsion methods, hardware and weaponry. It was also claimed that at least two aliens were kept at this site, in a habitat especially designed for the purpose. Further evidence came when Stevens unearthed the story of an unnamed Air Force pilot who cut across Area 51 while on a training exercise and spotted a circular aircraft about 20 metres across flying to the south of his own plane. Almost immediately he was ordered to land. When he did so, he was surrounded by plain-clothes investigators who questioned him for two days about what he had seen. Eventually they persuaded him that what he had observed was in fact a water tower. After signing a statement to this effect, the pilot was released. Shortly afterwards, he received a transfer to another squadron.

Strenuous efforts have been made to increase the security and inaccessibility of Area 51. In 1984 the Air Force simply annexed nearly 36,000 hectares of land adjoining the base. The perimeter is guarded by motion detectors, laser sensors, and groups of élite fighting men, formed into rapid reaction forces, who can reach any point in Area 51 within minutes. It has even been rumoured that personnel have the authority to shoot down civilian planes that do not heed warnings about invading Area 51 air space. Any top-secret military base is likely to be well guarded, but in time of peace and far from any possible enemy such precautions seem excessive.

The best first-hand account of Area 51 comes from American scientist Robert Lazar, who claims he worked in the highest security section, known as S4. 'The security was unbelievably oppressive,' says Lazar. 'There were security guards everywhere, following you all the time. There was never any free discussion allowed, which is the basis of good scientific research.'

Lazar caused a sensation when he revealed that he'd been ordered to investigate the propulsion system of captured alien spacecraft. This is how he described the UFOs he worked on:

> The UFO was very typical of what you would expect . . . two inverted dishes, and with a hump on the top. Metallic-looking, no wings, no fins, no visible propulsion system . . . Inside they were very sparse. If you came in the main entry way, you'd see three seats, the central reactor and wave guide that goes up to the ceiling, the three gravity amplifiers surrounding it – and you'd see just about nothing else. There's no wiring, no switches. There was nothing we would normally identify as a control surface. The seats and everything else in the craft were of smooth metal . . . as if carved out of wax. There were no right angles anywhere. Everything was one colour, a pewter grey colour.

Lazar said that the craft were too small for adult humans to enter comfortably, but looked as if they had been built for a creature the size of a child. His job was to work on the propulsion systems – to 'back engineer' them, trying to re-create the methods and materials used to build the finished product. His work was made difficult by the fact that the technology he was examining did not exist on Earth – nor, says Lazar, will it exist for a good many years. He describes it as:

> An advanced field gravity propulsion system, which in layman's terms means it doesn't have a jet exhaust or any kind of action-reaction system we're familiar with. What the device does is create its own

gravitational field which actually bends space and time around it. It does this by using a super-heavy element [known as element 115], one that we can't synthesize as yet. This element produces its own gravity wave that is amplified and applied directionally out of the bottom of the craft.

Lazar says there are two modes of travel for the craft. The first is for travelling around the surface of the planet by balancing on the gravitational field that the gravity generators put out. He compares it to a cork riding a wave on the ocean. The second is by bending space and time. This idea may be a bit unusual to some people, although it is perfectly familiar to atomic physicists. To give an analogy: if a thin rubber sheet is laid out on a table and pinned out at each corner (representing space time) and a pebble (representing the spacecraft) is placed at one end of the table, and a piece of the rubber sheet from another point is pinched and pulled up towards the pebble and then released, the pebble will follow the stretched rubber back towards that point. This analogy represents how the craft apparently manipulates space time around it. Lazar believes the craft do not use linear travel through space, but bend space and time as described here. If the sheet represents the space-time continuum, then it is possible to imagine how an object might thus precisely maintain its relationship with space and time, yet also move to an entirely different location.

Asked whether he had ever seen one of these craft in flight, Lazar replied: 'Very frequently. They were tested normally on Wednesday night, when the traffic was low in the area. I saw one test close up, and several from a distance of fifteen miles. On the one occasion when I was very close to it, the craft lifted off relatively silently, drifted over to the left, then to the right and sat back down again. It was fairly uneventful for a flying saucer.'

The authorities wasted no time in denying Lazar's claims; Lazar says they even tried to erase his identity. His story was originally revealed by George Knapp, a respected investigative reporter with KLAS TV in Las Vegas who subsequently went to considerable efforts to investigate whether Lazar was telling the truth. Knapp discovered that Lazar had worked at Los Alamos in New Mexico, the lab where the atomic bomb was invented. But Los Alamos flatly denied any knowledge of his existence. As far as they were concerned, he had never been anywhere near the lab. Knapp then confronted them with a phone book from the lab with Robert Lazar's name in it. Then they reluctantly admitted he had worked there in a minor capacity.

George Knapp then asked Lazar to take a polygraph (lie-detector) test. The polygraph examiner conducted a series of four different tests; three were inconclusive, but one judged that Bob was telling the truth about what he saw at Area 51, about seeing the flying saucers and working on anti-gravity propulsion systems.

Finally, Knapp arranged for a former employee at the base to quiz him for two hours – not about flying saucers and gravitational systems, but about the location of the cafeteria, the method of paying for meals, its decor, and so on. The employee was totally convinced that Robert Lazar really was at the base. Lazar's story has now been corroborated by more than a dozen people who George Knapp interviewed over the years. Although he has been ridiculed and attacked for telling his story, Lazar reckons that he did the right thing by going public. He claims that both he and his wife were threatened into staying silent, and believes that if he had not gone public, the threats would have been carried out. Lazar's cause has not been helped by the fact that his story has been exaggerated by others in certain quarters. Claims that he never made and firmly denies – that, for instance, he saw alien creatures at the base, and smuggled some of element 115 out – have cast doubt on his testimony and given ammunition to those who would like to discredit him. I certainly feel very open-minded about Lazar's story. 'Look,' he told me, 'I'm not interested in UFOs. I am interested in science.' Added to the fact that he has never made any real money from his experiences, and that a good investigative journalist has produced so many small pieces of evidence that, when added together, raise some important questions.

Certainly there is no doubt that the American military have been testing saucer-shaped craft, and mounds of documentation from many different sources show that they regard the possibility of alien presence in our universe as a serious one. For many years Area 51 has been the focus of so-called 'black projects', including the Stealth aircraft, and the weaponry developed under the Strategic Defense Initiative for use in outer space. Ostensibly, these were developed to protect America against earthly enemies; but was there a more urgent purpose behind President Reagan's 'Star Wars' project? He himself suggested that there might be: 'Perhaps we need some outside universal threat to make us recognize this common bond. I occasionally think how quickly our differences worldwide would vanish if we were facing an alien threat from outside this world.'

The unique footage we featured in the series showed an object following a Space Shuttle which had been launched into orbit. The picture flares in what looks like a magnetic pulse. In the next frames, it looks as if a missile or a laser weapon has been fired from Earth. The object changes direction, and accelerates away at what experts believe to be a speed of up to 900,000 miles an hour. Could it be that the object is a UFO taking evasive action from Star Wars missiles fired at it from earth? Many believe this is only the latest evidence of a continuing series of cover-ups of the real truth about UFOs.

Not all sightings that suggest the presence of alien intelligence in our universe are terrestrial. In 1976 NASA's *Viking* space probe came up with some unexpected results in its mission to photograph the surface of Mars – the planet most usually associated with the possibility of extraterrestrial life. The results re-ignited what had been a twenty-year controversy. Over 100,000 images were taken: one of them seemed to show five pyramids and a detailed likeness of a human face, in the Cydonia region of Mars. Richard Hoagland was consultant to the Goddard Space Flight Center at the time, and he recalls being told by his superiors at NASA that when further pictures were taken of the same area a few hours later, there was nothing to see. The face, they said, had been no more than a 'trick of the light'. At the time he was not suspicious, but he and other researchers into NASA activity have since realized that it would not have been possible to take pictures 'a few hours later', for the simple reason that this sector of Mars would by then have been plunged into darkness. Another Goddard employee, Vincent Di Piertro, subsequently come up with an image of the same spot taken a month later – but conveniently misfiled – which again clearly shows the image of a human face. It had not been a trick of light at all, but it seems that NASA had been quite prepared to cover it up. The episode seemed to be evidence that NASA does not want to reveal any discoveries of extraterrestrial life, as it might make for fear of the possible effect on humankind.

In fact Hoagland claimed in a recent interview:[1]

There are apparently two space programs. There's the space program we've all seen. And then there's the space program that the Brookings Institution warned NASA they shouldn't tell us about if they found certain things because it would destroy civilization. The Brookings Institution is a major think tank in Washington. It's been there for decades. It's composed of academics.

According to the paperwork, which we have, in 1959 when it was formed NASA turned to Brookings to basically lay out the outline of the space program. Brookings took a year and did an extremely extensive survey of all the areas that NASA might make discoveries in, ranging from weather modification to extraterrestrial life. In every area except one, Brookings recommended to NASA that it proceed full speed ahead.

1 In *Fate* magazine.

With regard to extraterrestrial life – Brookings recommends to NASA that it probably could find, in the [coming] years, evidence of other intelligent life in the solar system, either in the form of ruins or signals – they were talking about radio signals at that point. They then recommended that NASA give serious consideration to not telling anybody.

On December 15, 1960, the *New York Times* picked this story up and made it a full-page headline: 'Government Report Warns That Discoveries May Topple Civilization'. It is our belief now, compounded by additional evidence which comes in every day, that at that point the space program bifurcated – it became two programs, one in public that would keep us little kiddies sleeping quietly, and the other space programme that only a handful of the inner, inner sanctum ever got to see.

The mystery of the Face on Mars, and NASA's attempts to suppress it, caused a flurry of research into the Cydonia region, and Richard Hoagland and others have discovered many other puzzling features. The face itself appears to have an eyeball in the socket, a mouth full of teeth, and some kind of a head-dress resembling that of a sphinx. In the vicinity is a series of pyramid-shaped objects of massive size – the largest is thought to be over a mile across – which appears to have been laid out by some kind of intelligent life. Furthermore, the lines of the pyramids are so straight, and the angles so true, that it is almost inconceivable that they could have been created by accident. Another researcher, Ananda Sirisena, ran computer programs to calculate the probability of such geological arrangements happening by chance alone. The odds were little less than a staggering 200 million to one.

If this carefully planned structure is intended as some kind of message, what are its creators trying to say? The most compelling answers came when it was realized that the Cydonia pyramids and face bear an astonishing resemblance to the pyramids and sphinx at Giza in Egypt. Quite apart from the visual similarity, further research showed that the internal geometry of the two sets of monuments, their layout in relation to each other, their latitudial orientation, and their astronomical alignment are in each case almost identical. Over and above the astonishing evidence that such painstakingly created structures exist on Mars, it now appeared that these structures were almost a precise mirror image of one of Earth's most famous monuments.

The plot thickens when we look at a remarkable incident that happened to Joe McMonengle, who I will talk about more in the chapter on telepathy. Joe worked for the American intelligence services for over twenty years as a 'remote viewer'. That's someone with the psychic ability to visualize and describe distant places. One day Joe was given some map co-ordinates to target by NASA. He drew five pyramids and a sphinx. He thought that the co-ordinates were for a target on Earth and was almost as surprised as the people from NASA when he was told that he was targeting the Cydonia region of Mars. The most fascinating part of this target was that Joe believes he gained an insight into the history of the Martian pyramids. He says: 'Towards the end of the session I became aware of something else and it turned out it had a lot to do with who constructed the pyramids. I had a perception that it was a race of beings or humanoids that were sort of passing through at the time. My sense was they were moving through the solar system and had to move on to a different location and it's possible they moved here.'

NASA steadfastly refuses to investigate Cydonia further – or at least that is what it is saying in public.

It may be a long time before we will know the truth about Mars.

In Britain, where we have an Official *Secrets* Act rather than a Freedom of Information Act, the Ministry of Defence alternately tries to convince researchers that all records regarding UFOs have been destroyed, or that there was never anything worth looking at in the first place. As with ghosts and spirits from other planes of existence, I persist in thinking that the sheer weight of eyewitness evidence is overwhelming: it is not just a few cranks and nutcases, but people from all walks of life and in positions of authority and responsibility who can describe first-hand experience of UFOs.

The most suggestive and extraordinary (not to mention gruesome) UFO-related events are undoubtedly the animal mutilations I investigated in the first paranormal series. This is a subject which people find especially difficult to be objective about. We have evidence of literally thousands of mutilations, mainly of cattle but also of other large domestic mammals such as horses, sheep and goats; and we have the grisly remains themselves, proof that if a human hand is involved then a psychopath – or rather, an international con-

spiracy of psychopaths – must be at work. Linda How
Moulton has spent many years investigating anim:
mutilations, and her book *An Alien Harvest* is a quit
remarkable record of what has been happening.
describes what appears to be a systematic programm
carried out by alien beings to remove organs fro
domestic livestock – for what reasons we can onl
speculate.

It is difficult to know when these events began, bu
they seem to date back to the 1960s, and have occurre
pretty much wherever cattle are reared in isolate
places – from Australia and South America to the le:
populated areas of the United States. Typically, th
animal or animals in question are found dead and hav
had various organs removed from their bodies. Th
surgery has been performed with such precision th:
even expert pathologists do not know exactly how
was achieved. The state of the tissue around th
incisions suggests that intense heat has been applie
yet the flesh is not hard and brittle, as it would be
conventional heat had been the source. No one is quit
clear how many cases of animal mutilation there hav
been, but one estimate worked out in 1979 suggeste
that there had been over 10,000 such incidents *in th
USA alone*.

Organs chosen for removal include heart, live
spine, eyes, reproductive organs, rectum, digestiv
tract and lymphatic system, and whoever had bee
excising them knew exactly what they were after an
how to get at it. Most puzzling and macabre of all, i
the vast majority of cases the blood seems to have bee
drained from the carcass, and not one drop has bee
spilled. How it is possible to remove the heart from a

48

animal without leaving any trace of blood is a mystery which has not been solved.

Needless to say, those whose livestock have been mutilated are frightened and angry, and many are nervous of telling their story for fear of attack by whoever or whatever is mutilating the animals, and also because they don't want to be taken for paranoid fools. However, there are plenty of accounts to draw from.

What possible explanations are there for animal mutilations? The various theories are set out below:

1 The mutilations are the work of government agencies experimenting with biological warfare, who want us to believe that it is the work of aliens so that their efforts can be kept secret.
2 They are the result of the activities of natural scavengers, especially insects, small rodents and birds.
3 A cult is responsible – one that requires various sexual organs for the enactment of (presumably) satanic rituals.
4 The mutilations have been carried out by aliens who require the various organs for unknown purposes of their own, but perhaps associated with their own survival or with the creation of a servant race.

Each of these theories has its strengths and weaknesses. That government agencies are involved seems indisputable. Wherever in the USA a series of mutilations has occurred, it has nearly always been associated with high levels of covert activity: reconnaissance flights by unmarked helicopters, low-level passes by military aircraft, the presence of strangers in remote towns where visitors from elsewhere are very obvious, and so on. Very often people who have witnessed the results of mutilations have been visited by military personnel and questioned in detail about what they know.

However, one would expect the military authorities to be interested in such cases, especially where UFOs have apparently been sighted at the same time as a spate of mutilations has occurred. It is reasonable to suppose that by way of disinformation, military aircraft might be disguised with lights and luminous finishes to look like UFOs. What is less credible is that the authorities could think of no other way of assembling animal material for bio-warfare experiments, or any other kind of research. Would it not have been simpler to breed the livestock themselves, in secret if need be? And how come mutilations have occurred in nations where there is no known interest in biological weapons?

The 'natural scavenger' theory is the classic sceptic's response. Although in the majority of cases scavengers leave unmistakable signs of their activity behind – tooth marks, footprints, faecal matter, and so on – it is also true that some, especially birds, might not. Furthermore, certain scavengers regard various organs as delicacies and may go to great efforts to obtain them. If insects are involved, their scavenging might leave very neat excisions. And, of course, you would expect any carcass to be of interest to hungry animals, birds and insects in the vicinity.

So far so good. But too many questions are left unanswered. Most obviously, how did the cows die? Scavengers seldom kill their food. Predators do, but they would have to be large, and there would be evidence of how the killing took place – at the very least, bite marks around the neck. And what of the ample evidence that extreme heat had been applied along the incisions? And how did these predators or scavengers manage to exsanguinate (drain the blood from) their victims so expertly? And is it really likely that they would be quite so fussy over what they ate, and quite so precise in getting at it? Carcasses that have been scavenged are not uncommon on large farms or ranches, and they do not resemble the mutilated bodies at all.

The idea that a satanic cult is responsible seems even more far-fetched to me. Such a cult would not only have to be remarkably well organized at an international level, it would also need access to very large sums of money: for the expertise and equipment needed to perform what looks very much like laser surgery on the cows; and for the purchase and maintenance of aircraft. (Such a cult would have to have used aircraft of some kind – very likely helicopters – since there are typically no signs of human activity on the ground: no tyre or tread marks, and no footprints.) Again, why go to all that trouble and expense if a perfectly feasible alternative is to rear your own livestock? Lastly, no one has ever been caught in the act, despite the offer of substantial rewards.

Finally, we come to the suggestion that aliens are responsible. It is true that in a majority of cases there is no sign of alien involvement – no sightings of UFOs in the vicinity, and no circumstantial evidence at the site itself. However, in a significant number, scorch marks and flattened earth have been noted, as for instance in the case of a horse in southern California found with its skull stripped clean of all tissue, and its spine, brain and various other organs missing. Near by was a circular pattern of ten-centimetre-wide holes in the ground, and a number of round exhaust 'burns'. At various points in the vicinity, a higher than expected level of radiation was recorded. In another case, this time in Texas, concentric circles stamped into the rock-hard ground were identified near the carcass of a calf that had had its sexual organs removed. It emerged that a number of local residents had seen a strange orange light hovering over the ranch at about the same time as the mutilations occurred.

The Mexico State Police, which asked one of its officers to investigate the mutilations, could not deny that there was evidence of alien intervention. The officer in charge of the investigation, whose name was Gabriel Valdez, was studying a case in which a three-year-old cow had had its left ear, tongue, udders and rectum removed, and the cow's three-month-old calf had disappeared. Valdez noticed that an aircraft of some kind appeared to have landed twice near by. There were two sets of circular 'pod marks', set in a triangle, each of 18 centimetres in diameter. Leading off these triangles, which had a perimeter of 5 metres, were smaller sets of pod marks that had tracked the cow for about 200 metres. There was a cluster of pod marks near where the cow had fallen, and in various places scorch marks and a 'yellow oily substance' were found. This substance was sent to a laboratory for analysis, but apparently could not be identified.

In another case reported on by Officer Valdez, the remains of an eleven-month-old bull were sent for analysis. The carcass seemed to have been subjected to radiation of a kind sometimes used to kill animals but thought to be harmless to humans. It was dehydrated and the remaining organs, the heart and liver, were of a mushy consistency. Analysis (twice independently confirmed) showed that the bull's liver contained no copper and four times the expected amount of phosphorus and zinc. This particular carcass had broken bones and bruises suggesting it had been dropped back to the ground from some height. Not far from where it was found, circular 'pod-prints' were found – the ground was very dry and hard, so considerable downward force, or weight, must have been applied to make them. Valdez concluded that the animal had been removed by a hovering aircraft of some kind, mutilated, then dropped. 'Whoever is responsible for the mutilations is very well organized with boundless technology and financing and secrecy . . .' Valdez wrote in his report.

This conclusion is borne out by one of the very few eyewitness accounts we have of a cow being abducted. In Kansas in 1987 a farmer by the name of Alexander Hamilton reported that he had seen a UFO shaped like an airship floating above his land. He then watched in astonishment and horror as a grab on the end of a cable was lowered into his herd, and a cow was trapped in the jaws of the grab and winched back up into the hovering vessel. Only the hind legs and the head of the cow were recovered two days later on a neighbouring farm.

Another researcher, retired laboratory scientist Howard Burgess, noted that of the cases he had studied, 90 per cent were three- or four-year-old cows, or heifers of less than a year old. He wondered whether the cattle chosen had been marked in some way, and one night arranged with a New Mexico farmer to pass an affected herd one by one under ultraviolet lights of differing intensity. To the dismay of those present, three four-year-old cows and two heifers had vivid fluorescent 'splashes' on their backs. It was impossible to find a conventional explanation for these marks. The same night, an orange light was seen hovering over the lower slopes of a mountain a few miles away: two mutilated carcasses were found in the morning.

More than anything, it is the level of technical know-how and expertise that makes the 'alien theory' of animal mutilations so interesting. It is not at all clear that, even using the most advanced laser surgery techniques now available, excisions of this precision and neatness could be performed: with technology available in the 1960s, it is inconceivable. Equally impressive is the carefully managed use of radiation, a force which is notoriously difficult to control. Valdez believed that traces of radiation were being left to confuse investigators. And if radiation was used on the bull, then whoever applied it knew exactly what dose to apply to get the required effect.

Two people who claim to have first-hand experience of alien use of radiation are Betty Cash and Vickie Landrum. These two middle-aged women, together with Mrs Landrum's seven-year-old grandson, were driving along an empty desert road near Houston, Texas, when, they claim, a brilliantly illuminated diamond-shaped object came skimming low over the desert towards them. Flames seemed to be crackling around its underside. Hardly believing the evidence of her own eyes, Mrs Cash stopped the car and got out to watch. Mrs Landrum stayed in the car to comfort her grandson, who was by now screaming in terror. As she watched in amazement, Mrs Cash says she felt an intense wave of heat coming off the UFO, which was hovering perhaps fifty metres from where she had parked. After a couple of minutes, it slid silently away, following the course of the road along which the two women and the boy had been driving. Mrs Cash then reported that the UFO was joined by a squadron of helicopters, which she later identified as Chinook CH47s. This extraordinary procession continued along the road, with the car following, for a number of miles before finally disappearing over the horizon.

It was the most astonishing encounter, not least because it appeared to indicate co-operation between the UFO and the US military. But for the witnesses it turned out to have tragic consequences. All three rapidly developed a number of terrible symptoms: their skin blistered and broke open, and painful boils appeared in their scalps. Betty Cash was the worst affected. For weeks she suffered from violent fits of vomiting and diarrhoea. Her eyes swelled up and for a while she lost her sight. Not long after the incident, she developed breast cancer. The skin condition, which the hospital she attended in Houston could not diagnose, got worse and her hair began to fall out. She has never really recovered from her encounter, which – she is in no doubt – resulted in her receiving a massive dose of radiation.

Mrs Cash was so sure that the US military must have known about and even connived in the events of that day in 1980 that she sued them for $20 million, but lost on the grounds that the US military did not have in its possession any object remotely like the diamond-shaped vessel she described.

An incident like this confirms to some extent the view that aliens have business on our planet. Whether animal mutilations are a part of this overall plan, this profoundly disturbing story is far too well documented to ignore. Many writers have scrupulously amassed a hugely impressive body of evidence from a wide variety of sources.

3 The Psychic Detectives

British psychic detective Nella Jones claims a success rate of around 80 per cent and that she is regularly approached for help by police officers. At present, however, the British police force has no official policy regarding the use of psychic detectives.

The generally accepted view of paranormal phenomena is changing. It used to be assumed that only the lunatic fringe indulged in séances, hypnotism, spoonbending and the like. All sensible people, all rational people put their trust in science. Now, as we move towards the end of the millennium, people seem increasingly willing to set aside their preconceptions for a while and judge things on their merits. Alternative medicine flourishes, hypnotherapy is widely practised, and eminent scientists at some of the Western world's most venerable seats of learning spend their time trying to discover whether the human mind can affect physical objects by its own power alone.

Now, think of an establishment organization which of all establishment organizations seems least likely to be interested in such 'foolishness'. The police force would be an obvious candidate. And consider a rather arcane paranormal phenomenon, like the supposed ability some people have to envision events taking place in a different time and space, to read the past or foretell the future. You would have thought that these two would represent totally opposite poles of opinion: the one implacably imposed to such a nonsensical idea, the other equally certain that their mysterious powers are real – and never the twain shall meet.

But you would be wrong.

The people who would prove you wrong are called psychic detectives. They work alongside ordinary police officers, helping to solve crimes that might otherwise lie on the books for ever. Nobody really knows how they achieve their results, but the results are fascinating. The most famous psychic detective, Dorothy Allison, has now worked on over 4,000 cases, and in each and every one she has become involved only because of a direct appeal from the police. (Indeed, she will not even consider investigating a case unless the police or an official agency asks her to, and agrees to send a letter confirming the request.) After many years work, Dorothy Allison now has a large collection of letters from law-enforcement agencies across the United States, thanking her for her services and testifying to the invaluable assistance she has given.

In this chapter I will focus on the work of Dorothy Allison from New Jersey, and also Nella Jones, the British psychic who appeared on the programme and correctly identified the weapon used to attack the train driver during the Great Train Robbery of 1963. Neither woman is, of course, just a psychic detective: they claim their psychic abilities can be brought to bear on many different sets of circumstances; but it is their detective work that has made them famous, and in a sense has brought them into the mainstream of every-day life.

Dorothy Allison claims she has been psychic for as long as she can remember. She believes her mother was psychic, too, but she was also very religious and perhaps wary of anything that might be considered 'supernatural'. As a child, Dorothy lived in a world of 'pictures', vivid images that she says would pass into her mind, images of people, places, things. There was seldom any obvious rhyme or reason to the pictures: the ability to interpret and 'understand' their meaning came much later. Her mother believed that Dorothy Allison was psychic, and – unlike Rosemary Altea, for example, who was very frightened of psychic phenomena when she was young (see Chapter 1) – Dorothy Allison seems always to have felt comfortable with her 'encounters', even though they sometimes led to disturbing outcomes.

When she was fourteen, Dorothy was allowed to go to a dance held by the local church. She was about to leave when she noticed a strange thing: she believed she could see a wreath of flowers on the front door. She realized that the wreath was not real, but even so it upset her. Who was it for? Not long after seeing the wreath, she was sent out to the baker's to buy a cake, and this seemingly mundane event seemed to trigger a powerful feeling that her father was going to die.

As it happened, her father was in hospital. A heavy smoker, he had a bad cough and had been admitted for observation. But as an otherwise healthy fifty-year-old man there was never any real doubt that he would make a full recovery. Unknown to Dorothy, however, he had rolled off his bed, fallen awkwardly and broken a leg. Shortly afterwards he developed pneumonia. Already weakened by the cough and depressed and in pain from the broken leg, his condition worsened and he died.

When she grew up and left home and had a family of her own, Dorothy Allison seemed to have less time for her psychic work. Then, one day in 1967, she woke up very early after a horrible dream about a young schoolboy who had got stuck in a pipe. The boy was wearing a green snow suit, and his hair was swept to one side; she thought he was Polish. The dream was very powerful, haunting, and Dorothy felt she had to do something about it. She called other members of her family to check that their children were OK – they were. Then she called the police: at first they were sceptical, but they became increasingly interested as Dorothy described the boy she had seen in her dream. For the details she gave conformed exactly to details they had been given earlier of a little Polish boy called Michael, who had been out walking with his brother when he had slipped and fallen into the icy waters of the canal. He wore his hair swept over to one side and had been wearing a green snow suit. The police were trying to trace his body; although they had scoured the area, they were having no luck. Dorothy agreed to help.

She said she saw a school, and that the number 8 kept coming to her. Also, the number 120. There was a bend in the pipe where the body of the child was trapped, she was sure of that. And she saw a parking lot behind an ITT factory, and a lumber yard. And, more puzzlingly, gold . . . It didn't seem very promising: there was an ITT factory in town, but nowhere near the spot where the little boy had fallen into the canal. Not confident enough to insist, Dorothy tried to do what the police wanted her to, and spent long, weary days pacing the area where the boy had slipped and fallen into the chill, stagnant water. One day she was asked to walk around and stop when she came to the place where she thought the body of the boy was trapped in the pipe. She identified a possible place, but the city engineers insisted that there was no bend in the pipe just there. But the police ordered a hole to be dug, and sure enough there was a bend in the pipework. But there was still no sign of the little boy, no final, conclusive evidence of his death that would allow his distraught parents to come to terms with the tragedy and lay their young son to rest.

Dorothy was convinced the body would come to light on 7 February. The same numbers kept going round and round in her head: 8 and 120. But the police were getting nowhere with their search. They had restricted themselves to a three-mile radius, which seemed the largest conceivable area that a body could travel round the town's network of pipes and canals. To expand their search beyond that would in any case be impossible. It began to look as if they might never recover the body.

Come 7 February, no one expected very much. It was a mild day, milder than it had been all winter. Over the other side of town, near the ITT factory, water was beginning to trickle out of a defrosted pipe and into the river. As the day wore on, the trickle increased. And then the pipe disgorged its tragic burden, the body of the little Polish boy.

From where the pipe opened its mouth to the river,

you could see the parking lot at the ITT factory, and you were almost within the bounds of the local school, whose number was PF8. Michael's body was found at 1.20 p.m. But what of the gold? The casual onlooker might miss it, but there was a distinct gleam from the ground floor of an office building across the way. When the low winter sun caught it, something flashed. If you chose to look a little closer you would see, over the front door to the offices, the name of the lumber company whose yard was next door, painted on the glass in large letters of gold. Maybe a coincidence, maybe not.

The sceptics argue that some of Dorothy's predictions are very ambiguous, which is true. However, there are some that cannot be so easily explained. Often she is involved in locating bodies, but although she is sometimes distressed by the emotional content of her work, she does not, she says, ever share or experience the sufferings of the victims – and, indeed, she has little time for the histrionics of the type of stage psychic who claims to be forced to relive every gruelling second of this or that headline-making murder story. Interestingly she has chosen never to take money for what she does.

To an outsider, her method of working seems strange. Very often she says that it is during the phone call from the police describing the case and asking if she can help that she gets her most powerful insights. She says she has a sense for numbers, which are powerfully significant to her. She keeps careful note of any that are associated with the case, such as the age of the victim, and when she talks her conversation is peppered with numbers.

In February 1989 Dorothy Allison was contacted by a missing persons bureau in Colorado about a girl called Heather Church who had not been seen for five years. Immediately Dorothy said that the girl had been kidnapped by a man called Charles Browne – she was most specific about the 'e'. It turned out that a man called Robert Charles Browne was suspected by the police, but could not be prosecuted for lack of evidence. On the strength of Dorothy Allison's psychic insight, the police began to investigate Browne's past. They found that he had been in prison in New Orleans, and got fingerprints to compare with those found at the scene of the crime. They matched. Still they needed more. Dorothy Allison identified a tan car as the most likely source of incriminating evidence. So they began hunting for the tan car – and eventually found it. Even though it was by now several years since Heather Church's disappearance, traces of blood found in the car matched those of the girl, and at last Browne could be sent for trial.

As so often in the realm of the paranormal, we find an unwillingness to accept what we do not understand. If the truth be known, we cannot really explain or understand the very simplest forces at work in the universe: for instance, we know how electricity behaves and what it can do, but do we really know what it is? The same can be said of magnetism and gravity. And even when science does seem to have the answers, the answers only last until the next Newton or Leibniz or Einstein comes along and radically revises the entire intellectual edifice on which they were based.

For all that we know so little about psychic activity, perhaps we should try to distinguish the terms being used here. A blanket term often used is Extrasensory Perception (ESP), which means, literally, ways of gaining information independently of our senses. This term has been extended recently to general ESP (GESP), because it was felt that ESP might turn out to be too exclusive. We shall see later that, according to quantum theory, the act of perception or observation has an effect on whatever is being observed, so technically GESP can include psychokinesis (PK) as well. PK refers to the ability of the mind to alter the physical world without any intervention by a physical system (such as the muscular system), and in practice it is often investigated separately. Telepathy is a better-known term that refers to the ability to open a direct channel of communication between two or more minds, such that no physical medium is necessary for the communication to take place. Finally, clairvoyance describes the ability to see things that are separated from the viewer by time and space, and may also be on a different plane of existence. The work of psychic detectives are usually classed as clairvoyant.

Now, having carefully separated these phenomena, we ought to jumble them together again, because researchers have in practice found them well-nigh impossible to distinguish from one another. If telepathic contact is established, do the participants use PK to plant thoughts in each other's mind? If someone predicts by clairvoyance that something will happen, do they then use PK to make it happen? (This question makes life for PK researchers particularly difficult.) Once we are into this largely undiscovered realm, there is very little certainty, and hard scientific evidence is correspondingly difficult to pin down.

Nella Jones to some extent conforms to the public perception of what a clairvoyant should be like. Anyone who has witnessed her performance on television will know that she is a fascinating character, although she argues that everyone has psychic abilities within them.

Nella is a Romany, born and brought up in the Kentish village of Eynsford. In some ways her story mirrors that of Dorothy Allison: she believes she has had a 'sixth sense' ever since she was a child, and though she didn't always welcome the insights that came to her, she always felt at ease with what she calls her psychic sense.

Nella well remembers the first 'psychic' encounters as a child. There was an old woman who lived in her village, who could often be found leaning over her garden gate, talking to passers-by. Nella liked the old lady, and would stop to say hello. The old lady used to say that she was waiting for her son to get back from the war. Nella felt the sadness of her situation keenly, for she knew that the old lady's son was dead. She didn't understand *how* she knew: the knowledge was simply there. After talking to her one day, Nella felt a deep sense of sadness well up inside her. When her friend asked why she was being so gloomy, she told her that she was sad because the old lady was going to die. Everyone thought Nella was being silly, but then a week later, sure enough, the old lady did die.

What happened next must have been hard for a seven-year-old girl to understand. Suddenly, no one would talk to her, but crossed to the other side of the road if they saw her coming. Why? What had she done wrong? She managed to corner her best friend and ask her what was going on. It turned out that the story about Nella saying the old lady was going to die had got out, and now some people thought she was somehow responsible. *Nella is a witch*, went the whisper. From this time on Nella realized that there was something different about her, which made her vulnerable to the accusations of those who didn't understand her.

Nella Jones's first involvement in detective work came in a roundabout way. She had been watching a news item about the theft of Vermeer's painting *The Guitar Player* from Kenwood House in Hampstead, London. Nella had never been anywhere near Kenwood, but immediately a picture of the large, elegant white mansion came into her mind. She ran into her daughter's room for a pencil and paper and began to sketch: the house itself, the layout of the grounds, trees and, in particular, a wire-mesh fence. Also on the sketch map she put two crosses. When she had finished, she wondered what to do. In the past when she had had what she felt were insights into crimes that made the news she had always told herself it was none of her business and kept quiet. This time she decided to ring the police.

She was put through to Hampstead police station and spoke to the duty officer, explaining that she was clairvoyant and knew the whereabouts of some important clues in the Kenwood robbery. She told the officer what she knew, was thanked politely, and assumed that was the end of it.

However, the police very soon asked if she could give them further information and escorted her to London. Nella kept talking about the wire-mesh fence, while a highly sceptical police officer kept telling her there wasn't one. When they arrived at the scene, the fence was there all right, and Nella allowed herself to relish the disappointment on the sceptical policeman's face. Soon afterwards, they identified the spot marked on Nella's map, and there, lying in front of them, were the smashed pieces of the alarm system that had been attached to the back of the Vermeer. Neither the police nor their tracker dogs had been able to find it, but Nella had led them straight there.

Nella was now convinced that the painting had been hidden in a cemetery. When she said she also saw caves, the police went immediately to Highgate Cemetery, which houses a network of deserted catacombs. Nobody felt like searching such a spooky place there and then, even though Nella felt strongly that the painting had been taken there. But she was also driven to sketch a man's face. When she showed it to the police later, they immediately recognized a man who had been arrested for desecrating graves. No photograph of him had ever been published, but Nella's sketch bore a remarkable likeness.

Nella remained convinced that she was on the right track with her presentiment that the whereabouts of the Vermeer was associated with a graveyard. The painting was recovered – it turned up in the graveyard next to St Bartholomew's Hospital in the City of London. After that she would frequently get a visit from a policeman who would ask her the odd question.

*

The most famous case Nella was involved with was that of the Yorkshire Ripper. Unlike Dorothy Allison, Nella Jones believes she suffers from proximity to crime – suffers with the victims, and also suffers from dread and fear of the evil that drives murderers to kill. In the case of Peter Sutcliffe, this sense of dread was almost unbearable. Several times she believes she felt he was with her, so that she could see the cruel sneer on his face, the cold darkness of his eyes. For over a year his crimes oppressed her, as she suffered the awful frustration of feeling that she knew important and valuable information about him, but could not piece the details together correctly. Frequently she knew that he was about to strike, and when he did she felt sickened and utterly helpless.

Nella admits to being confused by this case, overwhelmed, perhaps. So what did she identify correctly about Peter Sutcliffe? She had always been convinced that he came from Bradford, and that proved to be correct.

Nella was also pretty sure that the man's name was Peter, that he was older than the police expected, that he had a beard, and that he worked as a long-distance lorry driver. She had seen his place of work, and accurately predicted how it would look. The letter C had seemed significant to her, and the company he worked for turned out to be called 'Clarks' – the name was written large on the side of his lorry. To her dismay, Nella also foretold that he would strike on the 17th or 27th of November, and the initials of his victim would be JH. Sutcliffe claimed the life of Jacqueline Hill on 17 November 1980. The name 'Ainsworth' also came to her shortly before the body of another victim was found in the grounds of a house belonging to a Bradford magistrate called Peter Ainsworth. In all these predictions, visions, psychic insights – call them what you will – Nella displayed an uncanny accuracy.

At the same time, Nella freely admits that she got some things wrong. The name Dinsdale kept coming to her. She saw a younger man than Sutcliffe, a man with a limp. Like the Ripper, he believed himself to be driven by religious fervour, and went round with a head full of cataclysmic visions of a fiery Judgement Day. For a while, Nella thought there must be two men involved in the murders – the older one with the beard and the younger man with the limp.

In 1981 a possible source for the errors surfaced. Peter Dinsdale was convicted and jailed for the killing of twenty-six people in arson attacks around Leeds, which was also Sutcliffe's hunting ground. Dinsdale had a limp, and frequently quoted hell-and-damnation passages from the Old Testament.

It would be wonderful if Nella could simply close her eyes and solve a crime, but she can't. For a start, the kinds of detail that come to her are often in some way symbolic, or picture-based; there are words and numbers too, but without context these may be difficult to interpret. Then there is the matter of time. In the world through which her insights seem to come, time has no meaning. In one case, Nella could not stop 'seeing' a double murder taking place in a Brighton antique shop: a couple killed in their bed by a man with an earring who set fire to their premises as he ran off. But no such murder had taken place. Two months later, a Brighton police officer spotted an antique shop on fire. The fire brigade was called and the fire put out.

In the flat upstairs, the bodies of a man and a woman were found. She had been battered to death, he had a knife in his back. Nella was contacted and asked if she could help find the murderer, and she directed them to Lewes market. And there they found him – but not until 1990, twelve years later. He has since been found guilty and sent to prison.

It is one thing to feel you know who committed a crime, but quite another to construct a case, amass the evidence, and get the perpetrator up before a judge. And in a way you can understand why the police, who have to put in all the legwork, sometimes seem reluctant to acknowledge the role a psychic detective has played in their investigation. To them it must seem as if the psychic will get all the glory while they get all the paperwork. But at times her job is also difficult.

She has been involved in many, many cases over the years, and the written testimony of the police officers she has assisted is very impressive (don't take my word for it, you will find them quoted in her fascinating autobiography). She once told two private investigators she was working with to cancel a trip to Belgium they had planned, and they had enough respect for her gifts to heed her warning. Just as well. The ship they were due to travel home on was the *Herald of Free Enterprise*, which sank with the loss of 200 lives.

We don't know very much about the nature and origins of psychic detection. The first description of the processes involved seems to have come from the American physiologist Joseph Buchanan, who believed that all things – including items we consider to be inanimate – have a kind of essence by which they express themselves. Embodied in that essence is the history of the object itself, and a skilled person can 'read' that history, interpret the aura. If objects really do contain a psychic imprint of this kind, then this would be a simple explanation of how Nella Jones was able to pick out the real weapon from among the fakes on TV. The process being described here may not be so very far from something with which we are all familiar: the feelings that can be associated with houses. Anyone who has been flat- or house-hunting knows what it is like to walk into a place you really don't like the feel of: you are hard put to explain it, but there is something uncomfortable . . . Conversely, some places just seem to be happy, vibrant and warm – and it isn't as if places that are clean and beautifully decorated necessarily feel great, while scruffy places necessarily feel bad. And to anyone who is sceptical about this, I would ask: would you want to live at 25 Cromwell Street, the house where Frederick and Rose West committed so many atrocities? And if not, why not?

It could be that any point of contact or association between a psychic and the perpetrator of a crime may be enough to trigger insights akin to those we feel in a house or flat, but perhaps in the case of the psychic the feelings are more detailed and better defined: images, ideas, numbers, words; the feeling of being there while a crime is committed, or of horrifying proximity to the criminal. As well as handling a piece of evidence, this point of contact could be a tour round the scene of a crime, or a conversation with someone who knew the criminal or the victim. Buchanan called his theory of the essence of physical objects 'psychometry'.

71

Arthur Conan Doyle, the creator of the great Sherlock Holmes (read his books carefully and you'll find that he nearly always solves cases on the basis of some mysterious intuition, rather than because the clues add up to the criminal) believed that the detectives of the future would be psychics. And today hundreds of people such as Nella Jones and Dorothy Allison work for police departments around the world – some of these departments even have written procedures giving guidelines about how officers should interpret information from psychics and use it in their investigations. A related development is that lawyers in the USA now sometimes employ psychics to help them select a jury which will be sympathetic to their client's case (there is an elaborate procedure for selection of juries in the United States). A survey in the *National Law Journal* in 1986 found that American lawyers foresaw increased use of psychics in legal work of all kinds.

Nella Jones and Dorothy Allison are two of the best-known psychic detectives, but there are many more. Carol Everett, for instance, who is based in Devon, works by providing detailed sketches of the people she believes to be responsible for various murders. In some cases it's been felt that these sketches prove to be better likenesses than photographs – and certainly far more recognizable than Identikit pictures. By May 1995, she had worked on no fewer than seventeen identifications for the police, including the murderer Gordon Topen, art thief Duncan Grey who stole paintings and jewellery from Buckingham Palace, and the woman who abducted baby Abbie in July 1994. In all of these cases Carol Everett drew the likenesses before the culprits were apprehended, and also supplied details regarding their whereabouts and the circumstances surrounding the crimes.

It is a pity that so few people are prepared even to investigate this area. Possibly some of the most fascinating and mysterious secrets of our universe are being ignored by scientists for no better reason than that they do not fit in with the current paradigm – the mind-set of the scientific community.

Perhaps some factions of the scientific community are frightened of what they cannot understand. But if you don't look beyond the boundaries of your mind-set, you will never discover anything that challenges or lies beyond it. Stuck in ever-decreasing circles of knowledge that can only perpetuate the systems and beliefs on which it is based.

Of course scientists have to persuade people to fund their research, and it isn't easy to convince people to make the big leap of faith needed to put money into paranormal research. And it is true that in some fields huge strides have been taken – see Chapter 5 on psychokinesis – but why is it so often for the military? But there is evidence that scientists who do stick their necks out and suggest that some of the subjects described in this book are worth investigating can be ostracized by their peers, made a subject of scorn and ridicule. Do people who cannot approach the unknown with an open mind, in a spirit of honest and enthusiastic inquiry, really deserve our respect, let alone our valuable research funds? It seems to me that what they are effectively saying is that they refuse to listen to anyone who challenges the orthodoxies on which their systems of belief are based – but let's remember that nearly every orthodox belief started life as a crazy theory that condemned its author to the fringes of scientific life.

4 Telepathy

A University of Chicago study revealed that 67 per cent of adult Americans believe they have experienced extrasensory perception (ESP).

Have you ever thought about someone, then shortly after the phone rings and it's them? Most people have had this experience. Is it telepathy, or just coincidence?

In this chapter we will look at premonition, precognition and morphic resonance, all more commonly known as telepathy. As I have already explained, telepathy is the ability to open a direct channel of communication between two or more minds in which no physical medium is necessary for the communication to take place. If this phenomenon exists, is there any reason why it could not be developed like any other human ability, so that trained telepathists could communicate as well as if they were having a normal conversation? This chapter introduces some people who have demonstrated remarkable telepathic powers, and also considers the scientific evidence that this ability really does exist.

The biologist Rupert Sheldrake – about whom more at the end of this chapter – has suggested that when we see something our eyesight reaches out and touches the object – intuitive feeling. Thus, if we stare at someone from behind we may actually be tickling the backs of their necks! Some informal studies suggest that 80 per cent of people believe that they do possess the ability to know when they are being stared at, or the ability to stare at someone and make them respond in some way. Sheldrake expresses his astonishment that no one has thought to investigate this mild form of telepathy any further.

Telepathy is closely related to various other phenomena that come under the heading of 'psychic abilities'. The point that I want to make is that 'psychic abilities' that we presently refer to are not very well defined. They do not sit in neat compartments, but overlap with one another; and it is to be expected that someone who shows abilities of one kind will also be able to develop other psychic skills. This has made research difficult. For instance, one of the classic experiments used to determine psychic ability is the card-guessing test, whereby the subject is asked to discern which card has been chosen from a set usually depicting various commonly recognized symbols. By comparing the results of a large number of such tests with the results that could have been expected from guesswork alone, researchers can decide whether the subject was using psychic abilities to identify the chosen card. The trouble is, exactly what is the identified ability? Is it precognition, the ability to foretell what card will be chosen? Or psychokinesis, the ability to influence the choice of card in some way? Or telepathy, the ability to read the mind of the chooser? Or perhaps some kind of extrasensory perception (ESP), whereby the subject identifies the card by 'reading' it without seeing it? Of course, the experiment can be varied to try to eliminate certain possibilities; but where we are dealing with mysterious phenomena, the results of even the most rigorously scientific procedures remain difficult to interpret. In consequence, parapsychologists have rather abandoned the old distinctions between clairvoyance – defined as the ability to see depictions of circumstances in a different time and/or place – and telepathy. They now look for general extrasensory perception (GESP), on the grounds that where our current state of knowledge is concerned, there is no useful distinction between the two.

Albert Ignatenko, the Ukrainian professor who appeared in the telepathy show, is another case in point. All of his demonstrations were amazing, including 'the psychic punch'. Whatever it was he hurled at our willing volunteer, it was sufficient to knock him right off balance. I was sceptical, but could feel something move past me. But what was the nature of the psychic communication here? Was it a thought along the lines of: 'You are losing your balance . . . You are falling over . . .'? If so, the thought must have communicated itself in an entirely non-verbal way, since Professor Ignatenko speaks no English and our volunteer no Ukrainian. Or was it simply a shaft of psychic energy. Certainly the weird, banshee-like wails emitted by Ignatenko as he prepared his subject and delivered the blow suggested a gathering and release of 'forces'.

Albert Ignatenko's ability to raise and lower the pulse of another volunteer in a different room indicated the ability to transmit something, but I wonder if telepathy was involved. Although the extraordinary Valeri Lavrinenko (see Chapter 7) demonstrated the ability to raise and lower his pulse at will, this is not a skill many people have, so even if Ignatenko had transmitted the thought, 'Lower your heartbeat', to the subject, how could he have responded? Maybe what we were actually witnessing was psychokinesis – the ability to use the power of the mind to affect physical entities. If so, then this particular power has frightening implications: if it were possible to learn to raise or lower a human heart to intolerable levels, or to stop it altogether, then it could be a dangerous skill in the wrong hands.

The term 'telepathy' was coined by W. H. Myers, who helped to found the Society for Psychical Research in London in 1882, and was one of the most enthusiastic researchers in the field. Whether you believe in it or not, the concept has a long and venerable history.

Some cultures associate telepathy with religion, and especially with mystical rituals. (This is true of other paranormal phenomena too.) Frequently, if an important decision had to be made in an American Indian village, it was expected that telepathic contact would be established with neighbouring tribes, although the form this took was subsumed in the larger process of achieving union with all things as the key to wisdom.

The medical profession has also been associated with telepathy. Most notably, Sigmund Freud, the father of psychoanalysis, found himself driven to distraction by unwanted insights into the minds of his patients. Concerned to develop a strictly 'scientific' methodology on which psychoanalysis could be founded, Freud could not ignore this phenomenon, but nor did he much care for its implications. Eventually he wrote it off as a manifestation of a crude and primitive means of communication that had largely been superseded in the course of human evolution by the more 'sophisticated' tools of language. Carl Jung also believed he experienced telepathic contact: he associated it with his belief that at an unconscious level we partake in experiences that are shared and common to all – the 'collective unconscious'.

Interest in telepathy has always been strong, but it reached a peak in Britain during the First World War. As the nation reeled from the shock of losing such a massive number of its young men to the seemingly senseless slaughter of the trenches, there were frequent reports that mothers, wives and sweethearts somehow knew about the death of their menfolk before the official letter arrived – and indeed this occurred so often that, in the turbulent atmosphere of the time, it was barely thought worthy of comment. The bereaved would turn anywhere for the consolation they craved, and some spiritualists who claimed they could put them in touch with their departed loved ones quickly took advantage.

After the war, experimental work in the field intensified. The most celebrated and dedicated of those who studied telepathy and ESP was J. B. Rhine, a botanist turned parapsychologist who was based at Duke University in South Carolina. Rhine was a fascinating character. To finance his studies, he sold pots and pans door to door.

Rhine developed a simple card-guessing test. His pack consisted of five each of five cards depicting symbols – cross, star, wavy lines, square and circle – making twenty-five cards in all. At its simplest, the method was for the researcher to look at each card in turn, while the subject described what was on it. In one session, they might run through the pack once, or several times. The average for each run would be five correct guesses. The first time Rhine conducted the test, however, he simply laid nine cards face down on the table. To his astonishment, it's claimed, his subject guessed every single one right. The odds against doing that are about two million to one.

It was some time before Rhine's next success – this time with a divinity student who Rhine claimed scored an average of nine correct guesses per run of twenty-five cards. Unfortunately, Rhine's methodology was still in its infancy. When Mark Hansel, a British professor of psychology, came over to investigate Rhine's claims that he was close to confirming the existence of ESP, he subjected the procedures used to test the divinity student, whose name was Hubert Pearce, to rigorous scrutiny. In order to preclude the possibility of Pearce catching sight of the cards, he had been asked to sit in the library while research staff in the laboratory went through the sequence of runs. But Hansel now demonstrated, by asking if he could be tested and scoring a sensational 22 out of 25, that is was possible for Pearce to nip out of the library, find a chair to stand on, peep through the crack at the top of the laboratory door, and read off the expected results. He could then get back to the library in time for the researchers to come and pick up his 'guesses'.

The controversy generated by this discovery dogged poor Rhine for the rest of his career. Already there were whisperings among the academic staff at Duke that the activities of this strange fellow – with his pack of cards ever ready to be whipped out of his pocket for a quick telepathy session – did not reflect well on the dignity and respectability of the university.

If people can prove that tests for telepathy may be faked, then it seems to be assumed that they have been. However, Hubert Pearce always denied that he had spent his hours as an experimental subject dashing from library to lab and back again, clambering on and off chairs and peering through cracks in the door. Why should he? His chosen career was as a minister of the church, where any psychic abilities might have been considered a black mark against his character rather than a cause for favourable treatment. Hansel clearly felt himself utterly vindicated in suggesting that Rhine's results were worthless. But the truth is that no experiment yet devised is completely proof against trickery. Of course, scientific rigour is important; but so too is an appreciation that even experiments that are theoretically flawed can have significant results.

The highly sophisticated tests now devised to test the closely related ability called psychokinesis will be explored in the next chapter, but there is one more influential test for telepathy that deserves a mention: the Ganzfeld test.

The name *Ganzfeld* comes from the German words for 'whole-field': an important principle behind the method is to try to get the subject's attention devoted seamlessly and entirely to the business of telepathy. The ideas that led to the development of this approach are interesting. In the first place it was claimed by Charles Honorton, who devised the method, that the kinds of signal on which telepathy is based are very weak compared with the kinds of signal the human body is used to receiving from the regular senses, and that therefore telepathic communication is likely to be very easily obliterated by slight sensory distraction: a car passing in the street, a chair scraping, a keyboard clattering. By the same token, he believed that people often had telepathic or ESP experiences while asleep and thus largely cut off from sensory input. Perhaps, then, ESP is much more common than we think, but is generally overwhelmed by ordinary sensory input.

Looking at the philosophy and practice of Hindu mystics, Honorton came across the notion of the *siddhi*. A *siddhi* is an unwanted image that comes to the person meditating as he or she attempts to clear the mind of all distractions as a prelude to achieving a pure meditative state of mystical or cosmic awareness. Honorton realized that the *siddhi* was very much akin to the ESP phenomena he was studying, an apparently unbidden arrival in the mind of something that has no obvious sensory source.

The common theme here is the state of mind of the subject: cleared of sensory distractions, relaxed, reflective, contemplative, almost asleep, in fact, but sufficiently awake to be able to exert control. Honorton reckoned that if he could get his subjects into this state, or something approaching it, he could get much stronger evidence of ESP effects than had hitherto been possible.

Initially Honorton worked as a team member at the Maimonides Community Health Center in New York, where research into dreams was conducted in the late 1960s and early 1970s. The studies aimed to find out whether the subjects – 'percipients' as they were called – could dream about pictures selected at random by the research team. By the time the project closed, they

had carried out 379 trials and accumulated 233 hits –
an impressive success rate. The statistical methods
used to evaluate the data were stringent, and the
likelihood of that success rate occurring by chance was
a quarter of a million to one.

The most remarkable result achieved by the Maimonides team concerned an Englishman named Malcolm
Beasent who claimed that he predicted the future in his
dreams. In what has now become a classic ESP
experiment, Beasent dreamed about a large concrete
building, about a patient escaping in a doctor's white
coat, about a hostile atmosphere, and a group of
doctors and nurses. When he woke in the morning,
the researchers began a complex series of randomizing
procedures on their collection of paintings and images.
When the process was complete, the picture chosen
was Van Gogh's *Hospital Corridor at St Rémy*. Beasent
had not only dreamed accurately about the pictorial
and emotional content of the painting, he had done so
before the painting had been chosen as the subject of the
experiment. What is more, Malcolm Beasent was able
to repeat this success several times during his stay at
Maimonides.

Honorton moved on to found the Psychophysical
Research Laboratories at Princeton, where the Ganzfeld test was perfected. In Ganzfeld the subject is asked
to place half ping-pong balls padded with cotton wool
over the eyes, settle into a relaxing chair, and listen to
'white noise' – a featureless sound rather like the
sound of waves lapping on a beach. The room in which
he or she sits is illuminated by a red light, which the
subject sees through the ping-pong balls as a uniform
pink glow. Under circumstances of mild sensory

deprivation, the brain soon ceases to attend to external sensory input, and the subject is then believed to be in a telepathically receptive state. An image is then chosen at random from a bank of 144, and the researcher concentrates on the image in an attempt to communicate its content to the percipient. Afterwards, the percipient is asked to describe the picture, and the accuracy of the description is scored.

Relatively cheap to put into practice, and offering a chance to carry out a repeatable experiment that has withstood assaults on its integrity and 'fake-ability', Ganzfeld tests have now been carried out across the world. What of the results? In 1985 an almighty row erupted in the scientific community about interpreting the data from forty-two published studies. Honorton claimed that they showed a 55 per cent hit rate, where – on his scoring methods – 5 per cent would have been average. *Nonsense!* declared psychologist Ray Hyman. Thirty per cent was nearer the mark; and when you discounted certain statistically anomalous studies, you ended up with nothing significant at all. *Rubbish!* countered Honorton. Even if you accepted Hyman's reasoning you got a 43 per cent success rate, at odds of over a billion to one.

Hyman then claimed that the results looked better than they were because tests that showed no ESP effect had been consigned to the bottom drawer of the filing cabinet; Honorton quickly demonstrated that for this objection to be significant, the bottom drawers of filing cabinets in research labs across the globe would have had to have developed positively Tardis-like qualities: to invalidate the published studies, fifteen times as many would have had to have remained unpublished.

When Christopher Scott and Robert Rosenthal, two of the most severe critics of ESP research, said that they were convinced by Honorton's arguments, it looked like game, set and match to the parapsychologists.

The victory appeared to be confirmed when the 1990 edition of *Introduction to Psychology* was published. By far the most important text in the field, *Introduction to Psychology* grandly defines the boundaries of its subject, declaring what is and is not deemed to be a proper subject for research. In past editions, parapsychology and ESP research had been given short shrift: now, to the astonishment of all who work in the field and are accustomed to dodging brickbats from the establishment, *Introduction to Psychology* admitted that the Ganzfeld results were 'worthy of careful consideration'.

The examples of telepathy so far examined have mostly taken place in the laboratory, and have been designed specifically to be repeatable, and to yield sets of data suitable for analysis by conventional means. But there are other kinds of telepathy too, and other ways of studying its effects. One of the most interesting is called 'remote viewing' and was demonstrated on the programme by Joe McMoneagle. Anyone who watched the show that night will have witnessed an experiment designed to see if Joe really could form a telepathic link with Shaw Taylor, who had agreed to act as the remote viewer's 'target' for the experiment.

Joe McMoneagle has a military background, and has worked extensively for US security services in investigations of telepathy. As a young man, he had no interest in the paranormal, and knew very little about the subject. He was a soldier, and like thousands of other men and women who make a career in the army, he lived a life heavily circumscribed by the demands and rigours of his profession. One day, while he was serving in southern Germany, he went to a bar with some army mates. They drank a bit, but Joe, who is a large, well-built man, was a long way from being drunk. He remembers feeling a bit strange, and getting up to leave the bar. But at some point between his seat and the door he passed out cold.

What happened next changed his life. For reasons which are still unclear, Joe very nearly died that day. And as he fluctuated between life and death, he believes he experienced a powerful near-death experience (NDE) of the kind reported by many who have found themselves delivered to the very borders of life: the feeling of separating from the body, of being peacefully aware of the commotion surrounding the death of the body, of moving on to a different plane of existence. The full experience is described in detail in Joe's fascinating autobiography *Mindtrek*. Joe believes he has never been the same since; most notably, it was after the experience that his psychic abilities emerged.

As he studied the picture of Shaw with which he had been supplied as an aid to concentration, Joe described the process he was going through:

> It's almost like tasting food . . . I'm just reaching out there mentally and tasting things. I'm trying to concentrate on him, perceive what it is he's looking at . . .

Shaw Taylor had no idea where he was going to go before he was handed the envelope, but it turned out to be Chelsea Bridge over the River Thames. It wasn't really highlighted in the film, but I noticed that the first element Joe drew on paper was a shallow arc, which to me looked identical in space and proportion to the long, low arches of the bridge. Of course, he also drew the river and the bridge over it. Sceptics will want me to point out that the bridge in the drawing had distinctive, upright pillars, which Chelsea Bridge does not. Against that, it does strike me as amazing that of all the items Joe could have drawn – a church, a stadium, a park, a railway station – he chose a bridge over the river.

Joe McMoneagle is impressively matter-of-fact about his extraordinary skill. He says he scores hits 25 to 28 per cent of the time (the 3 per cent are borderline cases). A 'hit' in his eyes means not just the odd accurate detail (he gets a detail right in over 80 per cent of cases), but a correct overall impression of the scene.

Disasters often seem to trigger a stream of precognitive telepathic events. For instance, in 1966 in Aberfan in Wales, a school was crushed by an avalanche of coal waste which, loosened by heavy rain, came thundering down from the mountain above the town, claiming the lives of 128 schoolchildren and 16 adults. On the evening before the tragedy, a service was taking place at a spiritualist church in Plymouth. One of the congregation had a vision of the events at Aberfan, which included the following description:

I saw an old school house nestling in a valley, then a
Welsh miner, then an avalanche of coal hurtling
down a mountainside. At the bottom of this
mountain of coal was a little boy with a long fringe
looking absolutely terrified to death. Then for quite a

while I saw rescue operations taking place. I had an impression that the little boy was left behind and survived. He looked so grief-stricken.

Even more poignant, one of the children who died had herself had a premonition of the impending disaster: two weeks earlier, as her mother recalled it, she had said: 'No, Mummy you must listen. I dreamt I went to school and there was no school there! Something black had come down all over it!'

In the aftermath of Aberfan, the London *Evening Standard* sponsored the setting up of the British Premonitions Bureau to look into these and other claims of precognition. Accounts of dreams, visions and warnings about the event were solicited, and of the hundreds of responses, sixty were considered worthy of further investigation; and of these, twenty-two were judged to have been genuinely inexplicable precognitions of Aberfan.

An even more astonishing story of precognition occurred in June 1974. Lesley Brennan was watching the Saturday-morning film on television at her house in Cleethorpes, near Grimsby on Humberside. The film was suddenly interrupted by a news flash: there had been a major disaster at the nearby chemical plant at Flixborough – an explosion had ripped through the site and many were feared dead. Shortly afterwards two friends came round and Mrs Brennan told them about the accident. They talked about it for a while, then forgot all about it until the early evening news. The explosion had happened at around five in the afternoon, the reporter announced. Mrs Brennan thought how idiotic TV journalists were to get such a simple fact so wrong: the disaster had occurred at midday, during the Saturday-morning film . . .

Yet when her morning paper arrived the next day, there it was in black and white. The Flixborough plant disaster had happened at precisely 4.53 p.m. – nearly five hours after Mrs Brennan had apparently seen the newsflash on television.

Meanwhile, the British Premonitions Bureau was receiving around a thousand reports a year, and the flow of stories showed no sign of abating. At one point, two people in particular seemed to be foretelling events with great regularity: a switchboard operator and a ballet teacher. However, as soon as they were investigated in more detail, their abilities waned. As far as the investigators were concerned, their precognitive powers were not in doubt, since many of their premonitions had been documented as having taken place before the event itself. But it seemed that once they started to take steps to apply those abilities consciously, they were no longer there to be applied. A sceptic might argue that this is ample evidence that the claims are nonsense – that, quite literally, they don't stand up to close investigation. On the other hand, there is possibly a parallel here with the receptive frame of mind invoked by the Ganzfeld test. Charles Honorton was certainly in no doubt that the subject of the test should be in an entirely relaxed frame of mind, free of the burden of conscious thought, halfway to sleep. Although this was not an absolute precondition of success, it may be that the 'noise' generated by conscious engagement with the external world was a severe hindrance.

Dean Radin of the University of Nevada has also

carried out some revealing studies in the power of precognition. In his experiments, subjects were placed in front of a computer screen and shown one of two categories of images, described as 'calm' and 'emotional' – the former being designed to induce relaxation, showing countryside views, the latter to induce emotional arousal, showing autopsies or pornography. While being tested, the physiology of the subjects was monitored continuously on a polygraph. Radin wanted to find out whether people could anticipate the state of arousal or relaxation before the image was displayed – whether in some way they 'knew' what category of picture was coming up next.

The results showed that people had a very strong precognitive ability with the emotional pictures, but little with the calm pictures. Radin believes that there is a good reason for this: human survival depends on getting as much advance warning as possible of impending disasters; we need such information in order to be able to take evasive action. But when something pleasant or agreeable is around the corner, the imperative to know about it isn't necessarily there.

There is also a theory, which admittedly is controversial, but which may begin to explain the power of telepathy and precognition. This theory makes an analogy with quantum physics: one of the abiding mysteries of that discipline is that particles are actually both discrete objects and waves, and that they partake of these two states simultaneously and indivisibly. By the same token, our conscious minds may be fixed and embodied in a particular temporal and spatial axis, while also partaking of a 'greater consciousness', one which is akin to what we call our unconscious and which Carl Jung described as being associated with certain symbols that had universal meaning for humankind. Could it be then that the unconscious is the interface with other dimensions, where we are not limited by time and space and which could therefore in theory allow us to see into the past and future and across any distance?

Could this be why people who appear to have telepathic abilities often have very little idea how they can tell the difference between a fantasy or flight of the imagination – which also originates in the unconscious mind – and something which is telepathic in nature? Members of the Cheyenne American Indian tribe believe that *language* is the telepathy of the left hemisphere of the brain, which is rational and logical and *telepathy* is the language of the right hemisphere of the brain, which harbours the creative processes of the human mind.

Despite the success of Honorton's Ganzfeld tests and the mass of anecdotal evidence that precognition is one form of ESP that is actually very common, many are not convinced that any such phenomenon actually exists. There are better, more logical explanations, they say, which have not been properly considered in the mad rush to make extravagant claims about bizarre paranormal powers. When we have dismissed all the possible explanations as impossible, then we can start to believe that something out of the ordinary is happening.

Christopher Scott has done some calculations on the subject of premonitions, and worked out that chance can account for a great deal. Consider, for instance, a characteristic premonitory dream about someone's impending death. When that person actually dies shortly afterwards, the dreamer is struck by the extraordinary accuracy of their dream – how did they do it? How did they *know* the death would occur? It seems impossible that it may have been a coincidence – after all, they may never have dreamed of a death before, and may never do so again. So it must have been a clairvoyant dream, demonstrating beyond doubt the presence of a paranormal ability.

Not so, according to Scott. By comparing the number of deaths that take place in Britain every day with the population as a whole, and basing the calculation on the assumption that having a dream about someone you know dying will happen to everyone once in a lifetime, he has worked out that once a fortnight somebody in Britain is likely to have an immediately accurate premonitory dream.

Or consider the possibility of having a dream about an air crash. It might be a particularly vivid and powerful dream, which haunts you as you go down to breakfast. You pick up the newspaper, start to read, and find out that there really *has* been an air crash – perhaps somewhere on the other side of the world, but a crash none the less. Do you assume that you dreamed it in advance? Don't. Think instead of the number of people dreaming about air disasters in Britain every night. Even if everyone only ever had one such dream, that would make over 2,000 air disaster dreams across the nation every night. Could all of them claim to have had a premonition if a disaster occurred the next day?

The fact is that probabilities are not that easy to assess accurately, and coincidences really do happen –

it would, indeed, be statistically 'impossible' for them not to, for if the chances are a thousand to one against and the event occurs ten thousand times, then there is a likelihood of the coincidence happening ten times. The classic example of a statistical 'miracle' is the answer to the question: How many people do you need to have at a party for there to be a strong likelihood that two of them will share the same birthday? The answer is that if there are forty-eight guests, then there is a 95 per cent chance. It would be like a huge coincidence if they met, but really it is nothing out of the ordinary.

Richard Wiseman did his Ph.D. at the Parapsychology Department at Edinburgh University under Professor Bob Morris. His subject was deception – an area he understands well because he is himself a professional magician. Richard has pointed out that many people depend for a living on fakery and trickery, and that parapsychologists are not necessarily any better at spotting it than anyone else. At Edinburgh they have identified five particular ways in which the psychology of deception can be applied to make observers, even highly trained scientists, believe what is not true, see what is not there – or, perhaps most importantly, miss what *is* there. Observers can be comprehensively fooled by:

1 Devices or tricks that deceive the senses
2 Devices or tricks that deceive the mind
3 Devices or tricks that deceive the memory
4 Devices or tricks that divert the attention
5 Wrong or untruthful information

A good magician or illusionist will have all five categories of trickery up the proverbial sleeve – and of course their professional and acknowledged skill is precisely to deceive the onlooker so that they believe something other than what really happened. Furthermore, the world of the magician is shrouded in secrecy: the Magic Circle regard it as very much in their interests to keep prying eyes from exposing the methods upon which their livelihood depends.

From the outside, then, there is often no discernible difference between the performance of a magician and the performance of someone believed to be psychic.

Ian Roland performed a faked telepathic reading on the show, and convinced many people that he had miraculous powers. Generally there are three categories of such readings. The first, a 'hot' reading, is just plain cheating: the 'psychic' ensures that he or she keeps clients in the waiting room before the reading, and while there has someone go through their pockets for clues, question them directly about their lives, and generally garner as many details as possible. This information is then fed back to the astonished and admiring client.

'Warm ' reading involves asking direct questions of the subject, but at the same time disguising the questions, making it seem as if the answers are coming from the 'psychic' rather than the client. One technique used is to respond to the questions by repeated use of such phrases as 'Yes, exactly', 'Just as I thought', 'I know you are' and, more brazenly, 'Didn't I say just that earlier?' or 'Don't tell me, I already know the answer to that one' (followed by rapid change of subject, or perhaps a piece of outrageous flattery to divert the attention!). Another technique is to phrase questions rhetorically (as in, 'I am wondering whether you are fond of animals . . .') – the yes or no that follows will frequently be followed by a stream of other clues. If the subject is sufficiently relaxed and wants to believe in the powers of the reader (as most do), information may be freely volunteered. It may be the case that the reader's client is only there in the first place because of a desire or need to talk to someone neutral about a tragedy or problem or difficulty in their life. In this case, the psychic's task is made even easier.

'Cold' reading is the technique used at large gatherings or fairgrounds, when the psychic reader knows nothing about the subjects but must read their minds on the spot. This is acknowledged to be very skilful, and techniques for carrying it out have been accumulated and passed on for centuries in families with a tradition of doing readings for a living. In addition, cold reading requires instant assimilation of visual clues: age, style of dress and hair, accent, complexion, a wedding ring, an expensive watch, a tattoo – all can be revealing. For instance, if someone is wearing a wedding ring it is easy enough to say, 'The family is very important in your life, is it not?' Or if someone is tanned, the suggestion 'I see travel to faraway places' may be a good starting point. The trick is to get the conversation going, for the client will soon reveal enough to make the reading a success: especially if, as in the majority of cases, the subject is either there for fun and can easily be satisfied, or has come with some specific purpose which they will be unlikely to keep hidden. If the worst comes to the worst, the reader can always resort to the classic, 'I'm getting confused signals, can you help me out here?'

By way of advice, cold readers like to make so-called

'Barnum statements'. These are personality descriptions or pieces of advice, which people are inclined to think apply exclusively to themselves but which in fact hold good for the vast majority of the population. There are numerous lists of such statements available, but here are nine of the best:

1 You have a tough exterior, but deep down you are quite tender and sensitive.
2 You have a strong desire to be liked and respected by other people.
3 You tend to be too harsh on yourself.
4 You pride yourself on being an independent thinker.
5 There are times when your working life is very stressful.
6 You are strongly idealistic and sometimes feel let down when people don't live up to your expectations.
7 Often you are friendly and outgoing, but sometimes you turn in on yourself and seem introverted and reserved.
8 You have a tendency to worry about money; financial security is very important to you.
9 You feel that you have plenty of talent and potential that hasn't been fulfilled.

These types of statement are used daily in newspaper astrology features.

Anyone could add their own questions to this list. On the spur of the moment, they seem like wonderful, spontaneous insights into your hidden nature; in the cold light of day they look plain dull. The skill is in asking questions that confirm your basically good opinion of yourself (4, 6, 9), allow you to adapt the question to your own character (3), or cover all eventualities anyway.

When conducting a stage performance, readers will throw out questions likely to identify someone in the audience. 'I'm getting a John, a Jones, a James or a Jeff, who has passed away, does that name make sense to anyone here?' Then they move on to more ambiguous categories, for example: 'I'm getting a foreign country', or 'I see a uniform'. These generalizations could apply to almost anyone, and usually do to the vulnerable recently bereaved, who desperately need to make these 'psychic' messages fit.

The skill of the cold reader may be judged by the difference between the client or subject's account of the reading and a sober assessment of what actually took place. In a TV series hosted by arch sceptic James Randi, which aimed to debunk paranormal phenomena, one man was asked how many names had been mentioned during the course of the reading. So far as he could remember, the medium had mentioned only a few names, all of which had been correct. Video evidence revealed that if you counted in variations on names, the total number mentioned was over thirty! Whether you believe that cold reading is a bit of harmless fun which may sometimes serve a useful therapeutic purpose, or iniquitous fakery which exploits the gullible and can give them a totally false notion of reality, the skill of its best practitioners leaves many unanswered questions.

So, the debate rages on. Some of the most intriguing suggestions as to how definitive experiments testing telepathic ability could be devised and implemented have been suggested by biologist Rupert Sheldrake in his book *Seven Experiments That Could Change the World*.

Sheldrake's interest in the subject began with observations of the animal world. He was interested in the problem of identifying how pigeons homed in on their own lofts, which has defied all attempts to find a conventional explanation. Animal behaviourists have considered numerous possibilities: that pigeons innately record the twists and turns of the outward journey and reverse it to get home, or that they follow a series of landmarks; that they navigate by the sun, or by atmospheric light conditions; that they use their sense of smell, or detect the Earth's magnetic field. But none of them answers every example of a pigeon's remarkable ability to find its loft. Whether battered by violent storms, flying in thick cloud or pitch darkness, driven by car to an unknown destination before being released, sent off with their sense of smell blotted out or magnets attached to their feet – the pigeon always seems to find its way home.

Rupert also investigated the termite. Totally devoid of any apparent means of communicating with its neighbours (the termite has no sense organs), colonies of termites nevertheless manage to build the most complex imaginable nests, cathedrals of the insect world. How are the activities of the thousands of individual insects co-ordinated to achieve this feat of architecture and engineering, he asks. And who holds the overall plans that they manage to follow with such accuracy?

Another example: in the Second World War, milk

The show is always filmed in front of a 'live' audience, although some of the ghosts would probably disagree.

The fascinating Eddie Burks describing his investigation of the haunting of a pub in Oxted, Surrey.

Leo May who believes his voice is a channel for the legendary Italian tenor Enrico Caruso. A spectogram comparison of their voices did show a remarkable similarity.

Psychic detective Nella Jones examining various weapons. The pickaxe handle she is holding is the one used in the Great Train Robbery. Nell identifies it correctly first time.

Ukranian professor Albert Ignatenko demonstrates
his incredible 'psychic punch'. The willing volunteer:
going . . . going . . . gone.

Photograph by Swiss farmer Billy Meier on 8 March 1975. Bob Lazar says Meier's photographs bear a close resemblance to the craft he claims to have worked on at Area 51.

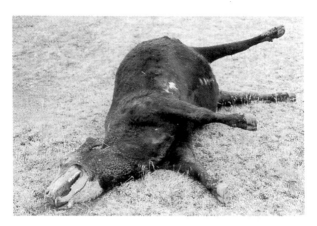

Steer found in Caldwell, Kansas, in 1992. Jaw, flesh, bone and teeth had been excised in bloodless, oval cuts. A pathologist's report stated the excisions had been cut with heat hot enough to cook the haemoglobin.

Linda Moulton Howe (right) explains the astounding mystery of the cattle mutilations. Timothy Good (centre), Britain's most respected UFO researcher.

This place doesn't exist, but this Russian satellite photograph tells another story. Note the huge runway. Area 51 is the home of America's 'black projects'; the Stealth technology was developed here.

Scientist Bob Lazar who caused outrage when he claimed that he worked for the US Government on extraterrestrial spacecraft.

The remarkable Joe McMoneagle whose ability to
'remote view' distant places with uncanny accuracy
makes him an extraordinary man.

The renowned bio-energy healer Seka Nikolic also appeared on the programme.

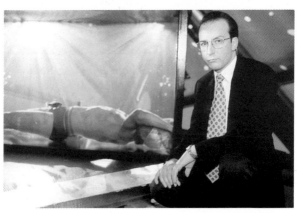

Russian superhuman Valeri Lavrinenko remained underwater for nearly seven minutes without breathing.

bottles were withdrawn in the Netherlands as an economy measure, thereby depriving blue tits of their morning cream. When the war was over – that is to say, several generations of blue tits later – the little birds took up this activity again as if they had never stopped. How do the new generation get the notion that the tinfoil caps hide a drink of milk?

As a result of his interest in such evidence of inexplicable powers in animal communities, Sheldrake also became interested in some of the remarkable stories about animals which appear to have psychic powers.

The indefatigable J. B. Rhine was one of many who researched this area, and he concluded that animals may possess five types of psychic ability:

The ability to find the way home.

The ability to locate masters or mistresses even if they are not at home.

The ability to sense the impending return of a beloved master or mistress.

The ability to sense impending danger.

The ability to sense at a distance the injury or death of a beloved human or creature.

The homing ability is shown in its most extraordinary form by homing pigeons, while the related ability to locate a human master wherever he is, though less common, has been found, for instance, when pets left behind in a house-move manage to find their family again, without any obvious means of doing so. The ability to foretell a homecoming was amply demonstrated by JT, the dog which starred on the show we did on telepathy. Viewers saw how Pam (JT's owner) was taken off by a researcher, leaving JT behind. Pam had no idea when she was going to return. A camera was trained on JT, who spent most of the time asleep. But within four seconds of the moment the researcher announced to Pam that it was time to go home, JT's ears pricked up and he padded over to the window to wait. And when her return was imminent – but before he would possibly have heard or smelt a car approaching – he showed unmistakable signs of anticipating a joyful homecoming.

The ability to sense danger has also been widely recognized. During the Battle of Britain, many people took to observing their cats closely as dusk approached. If the cat's fur stood on end and it dashed for cover, an air-raid was imminent. Anyone who lives in a part of the world that is prone to earthquakes would also do well to heed the behaviour of their animal neighbours, since quakes in Agadir, Morocco, Skopje in Macedonia, and Tashkent in Uzbekistan were all preceded by a mass animal exodus. One Canadian study seemed to demonstrate this ability in the laboratory: researchers observed the behaviour of a group of rats that was subsequently divided at random into two, with one half of the group being killed. Those rats that were killed had shown markedly increased activity as their end approached, even though no one at the time knew which rats were going to be selected.

Various experiments have suggested strongly that animals do communicate telepathically at times of crisis. In one, a boxer dog which had been wired up to a heart monitor experienced a convulsive heartbeat when its owner was subjected to abusive threats in another room. In a rather objectionable test carried out

n the former Soviet Union, researchers found that a
nother rabbit separated from its young reacted
trongly each time one of the young rabbits was killed.
n order to provide an impenetrable barrier to any
nown method of communication between mother
nd young, the young were taken down in a sub-
narine.

Sheldrake's belief is that phenomena such as these
night be explained by the existence of 'morphic fields'.
Ve are quite familiar with the idea of fields from
tudying such forces as magnetism, light and gravity,
ach of which plays around the source of its particular
ind of energy, be it a magnet, or a light bulb, or the
arth itself. He believes the key quality of a field is that
t is 'holistic' – it cannot be broken into component
arts and studied in the mechanistic way espoused by
onventional science, but is whole in itself. In genetics
uch fields are used to describe the way identical genes
an produce different parts of the same whole – in the
uman body, for instance, the morphogenetic field
ontains the overall plan to which the individual genes
espond.

But the morphic field is not fixed. Rather, it evolves
onstantly by means of a process Sheldrake calls
morphic resonance', whereby those elements that
ake part in the whole and follow the overall plan it
mbodies also shape its future development. This idea
lso relates to concepts in quantum physics, which will
e looked at in greater detail in the chapter on
sychokinesis: the observation, for instance, that sand
rickled through a narrow opening will fall at random
ntil a certain volume has passed through, when some
ind of organizing influence exerts control and the

sand forms a neat cone, with grains cascading uniformly down its sides.

The termite's nest is an example of a morphic field in action. Formed by the influence of like upon like, of termite upon termite, it exerts its organizing influence in the construction of the nest and develops according to the further resonance created by the activities of the colony. The homing pigeon might, by the same token, share a morphic field with its kin back home in the loft, and Sheldrake has suggested ingenious experiments to test this hypothesis. A morphic field might also, in the case of the blue tits, embody the information that sustenance could be had from milk bottle: but because the field is not dependent on one or a group of members of the flock but is a common memory store created from the moment the flock reached a certain number, it easily survives the passage of generations intact.

The larger question is whether, if they could be proved to exist, morphic fields could possibly account for the whole range of telepathic or clairvoyant communications. It is certainly an attractive theory, and one which seems well suited to the experimental approach Rupert Sheldrake proposes. And a further fascinating question lies beyond: what is the precise nature of the bond that unites the animals or people who share a morphic field? We are a long way from finding the answer to such questions, but is it too speculative to wonder whether we should be looking at some of the characteristics that already bind such groups together: in the case of a flock of birds, for instance, the sense that the survival of the one is inextricably linked with the survival of the many. It has already been observed that among humans and between humans and their pets, a bond of love may be a powerful facilitating force in telepathic communications.

5 Psychokinesis

Considering his own relationship with the sum total of all knowledge, Isaac Newton described himself as, 'a little boy, playing on the seashore and diverting myself now and then finding a smoother pebble or a prettier shell than ordinary, while the great ocean of truth lay undiscovered all about me'.

Research in the field of psychokinesis seems to relate to discoveries on the very fringes of mathematics, physics and philosophy. These discoveries are grouped under the term 'quantum theory'. As yet they are barely understood, and are very far from yielding up all their mysteries to the Newtons of our age. But if they ever do, then research into such subjects as psychokinesis may have a vital part to play in a process which has the potential to revolutionize our view of how the universe operates – and hence to have an effect on every corner of our lives, just as the Industrial Revolution changed the lives of all who lived through it.

Psychokinesis, or PK as it has come to be known in research circles, refers to the ability of the mind to affect physical objects remotely: that is, without the intervention of the body's muscular system. The classic and perhaps most widely observed example is of a clock stopping when there is a death in the house – as if there were some invisible link between the dead person and the mechanism of the clock, such that when the link is broken, the clock breaks down. But psychokinesis extends much further than this. Levitation, some forms of psychic or spiritual healing, metal-bending, affecting the outcome of rolls of the dice or computer-generated sequences of numbers: these are all examples of PK. It can apparently occur spontaneously, without conscious volition on the part of the subject, or it can be deliberate and consciously applied.

For an example of the latter, look no further than the experiment with the National Lottery we did in the first series. You may remember that we asked Camelot if we could borrow one of their machines, which they initially agreed to. However, when they discovered that we planned to use it in a mass PK experiment they withdrew all support and registered their strong disapproval of the experiment. So we mocked up a National Lottery draw to select a set of numbers, then asked all our viewers to concentrate on the numbers we had chosen while watching the real draw on the following Saturday. The result? Three of the pre-selected numbers came up.

Coincidence? Or psychokinesis?

Lottery operators Camelot may have thought there was a lot more to it than that. Only a week after our three numbers came up, they changed the rules of the game so that people who got three numbers right wouldn't any longer be guaranteed ten pounds if there wasn't enough money in the pot that week to pay them all. We rang Camelot to ask them if it was our experiment that had prompted this decision. Absolutely not, came the reply. Pure coincidence, then? Judge for yourself . . .

Potentially, we have a huge area of study. At one end of the scale, it is possible to say that the ability of the mind to control the body is essentially psychokinetic. When we place one foot in front of the other in repetitive sequence, or pick up a pen and write, or direct and focus our eyes at something that interests us – to name but three of the thousands of activities of which the human body is capable – we do so at the behest of our minds, which co-ordinate, collate and record such activities in a staggeringly complex sequence of computations that continues until the day we die. Medical researchers know a certain amount about how the mind sends instructions to the body's physical systems to make it operate as required, but very little indeed about how those instructions are generated. The objection to this viewpoint is that the brain is itself a physical system, which is physically connected to the systems it controls: there is nothing mysterious about the transference of instructions, because we know it is carried out by 'pulses' transported around the central nervous system. However, it remains true to say that there must be a level of abstraction somewhere in the human command system: how else could we make conscious decisions based on calculating the possible results of various options, or sift back through our memories of the past, or use our imaginations? Then the original question remains: by what process are abstract thinking processes translated into instructions that can be accepted and acted upon by the physical systems of the body?

At the other end of the spectrum, we have a notion borrowed from the world of quantum physics that states that if information is extracted from something then that something is itself altered by the process of extraction. In everyday terms it means that because at a subatomic level all things are in perpetual and indeterminate motion (they are 'fuzzy' as the jargon has it), then to observe something is to fix it at a particular instant, and hence to impose a particular measurement upon it, selecting from the range of possible measurements implied by its essential 'fuzziness'. Because of this, any form of ESP or telepathy or clairvoyance is a form of psychokinesis, since it is extracting information from an object and hence defining it in a particular way. Even more significant, when that object is defined by observation, any other object to which it is related will have to be defined along the same lines. Since these relationships stretch across time and space, then by implication the act of observation may do likewise. It looks as if we have, in outline at least, a theoretical basis in quantum physics for psychokinetic effects.

If this seems a somewhat unusual concept, then rest assured that the finest minds in the world are still grappling with its practical implications! My purpose here is to show that the continuum of PK activity begins at one end with something that is experienced by everyone (the ability of the mind to control the body) and ends at the other by embracing all forms of psychic power and connecting with some heady concepts of modern physics into the bargain. Psychokinesis may in fact be the mother of all paranormal phenomena.

Other chapters in this book consider healing, telepathy, psychic detection and clairvoyance, and evidence that the power of the mind can be harnessed to help the body act in apparently superhuman ways. To some extent, psychokinesis plays a key role in all these activities. However, in this chapter I will concentrate on the more familiar forms of PK such as metal-bending and attempting to influence rolls of the dice, and will also try to cover the laboratory work that has been carried out on what are called 'micro-PK' effects: the ability of the human mind to influence small-scale elements in mechanical processes in ways that are not visible but that can readily be subjected to sophisticated statistical analysis, and are therefore of special interest to researchers.

PK research has revealed that belief in the phenomenon (faith) is an important facilitator, and that in general people who believe (referred to as 'sheep' in the jargon) do better than sceptics ('goats'). On this evidence, one might expect people with a strong faith to be better at reproducing PK effects than those without.

A truly extraordinary set of experiments took place in the seventies in Canada under the auspices of the Toronto Society for Psychical Research. The experiments were carried out by members of the society who met regularly over a two-year period to make contact with a spirit known to them as 'Philip'. The sessions were filmed and, over time, the group developed an extraordinary rapport. It's claimed they were able to summon 'Philip' almost immediately and persuade him to carry out a variety of PK activities, including knocking on the table, answering their questions by use of coded knocks, and even tipping the table up as the group's hands rested on it from above. On one occasion, it's claimed, one leg only of the table around which they were gathered lifted off the floor, leaving the other three on the floor: there was the sound of wood and metal being twisted out of shape, and it seemed certain that the table would break. Apparently it took four of the group pushing hard down on the raised corner to push the surface flat again. Close examination of the film is *not* conclusive as to whether the participants in the experiment are lifting the table. However, later that night, sweets were passed round. Out of courtesy, Philip was also offered some, which were placed on the table for him to come and get if he would – or could. As a tease, one of the group reached out to take Philip's sweets, and, it's claimed, immediately the table tipped up at an angle of forty-five degrees – and yet the sweets stayed exactly where they were on the table. Several other people put sweets next to Philip's, and they didn't slide down the table either.

Apparently it took several more months of cajoling before Philip was prepared to perform a full-scale levitation on the table, but when it finally occurred, it was a moment of great triumph for the group.

In itself this is a remarkable enough story. But there is a special twist. 'Philip' did not exist. He was invented by the group as the means by which their shared purpose could be explored and achieved. They named him, they gave him this character, they carried out possibly by psychokinetic means every action he performed. But why?

The answer is that they were attempting to create conditions favourable to the generation of PK events. It had often been noted that in group sessions individuals were fearful that they might interfere with group intentions by producing effects of their own. Further, they believed that the more 'serious' and 'scientific' a session became, the less likely it was that any PK energy could be harnessed and used. Finally, it was nearly always the case that after a successful sitting, the following sessions would be dismal failures. The cause of this might have been that the groups in question became overconfident in their own abilities; or, conversely, that they were so shocked by what had happened that they blocked attempts to do the same thing again. At any rate, the invention of Philip proved an inspired answer to these obstacles. A focus for their efforts as a group, he also enabled them to develop a light-hearted, bantering atmosphere, and allowed them to stand at one remove from the events they were possibly causing themselves.

Our own century, too, has produced some outstanding exponents of the art of psychokinesis. One who deserves to be better known is Nina Kulagina – a film of her breaking a cord using willpower alone was shown on the programme about PK. It had long been known that both the Russians and the Chinese had been conducting extensive research into psychic phenomena, and in the West, at the height of the Cold War, there was nervousness that the Communist nations might have discovered something important – something, at worst, with military applications that would tip the delicate military balance in favour of the Eastern bloc. The Russians fuelled Western paranoia on the subject by guarding Kulagina closely. However, in 1970, two noted Western parapsychologists managed to arrange a brief experimental session with her in a hotel in Leningrad.

What Champe Ransom a researcher at the University of Virginia) and his colleague Gaither Pratt saw confirmed much of what had been said about her.

Kulagina impressed everyone with her matter-of-fact approach: there were no histrionics, no last-minute refusals – she agreed to whatever was suggested, and submitted to whatever tests and safeguards were deemed necessary with total equanimity. On this occasion, the two Western scientists watched in awe as Kulagina performed a warm-up routine, which involved stretching out her hands towards a matchbox on the table before her, and making it move towards her. Next, Ransom placed a handful of aquarium gravel on the table, spread it out, then placed a cylinder made of a non-magnetic material in the middle of the patch of gravel. Finally, he put a glass over the cylinder. When asked, Kulagina concentrated, and moved the cylinder through the gravel, leaving a distinct trail behind it, until it bumped up against the edge of the glass. When the glass was removed, the cylinder resumed its eerie journey across the circle of gravel.

Kulagina's abilities have been extensively researched and documented by Soviet scientists. She has been filmed apparently lowering and finally stopping the beat of a frog's heart, apparently levitating objects, and moving several objects on a table in different directions. The aim of much of this analysis was to identify what advanced form of trickery Kulagina was using, for in the Soviet Union at this time scientists were even more ferociously rationalistic and mechanistic in their approach than their Western counterparts. She was investigated by the Institute of Precise Mechanics and Optics and the Baumann College of Higher Technology in Moscow, and the Institute of Radio Engineering and Electronics in Leningrad. As their star performer, Kulagina must have gone through some very arduous tests, and, given that the usual treatment for people who annoyed the Soviet authorities at that time was imprisonment or death, it would have taken a brave, not to say foolhardy woman to practise such extended deception on teams of eminent research scientists.

One of the most notable results of the research that was Kulagina found the exercise of her PK abilities physically very demanding. When moving objects, her pulse rate would rise dramatically. As you would expect from someone expending that kind of energy, her blood sugar levels also rose, and, it's claimed, she would lose up to three pounds in weight during a typical session. Despite this, she never refused at least to try to move objects put in front of her. When the British physicist Benson Herbert visited her in 1973, Kulagina said she felt too unwell to take part in the experiments. However, sitting in a chair several feet away from the apparatus Herbert had erected – which included an electrically grounded screen, a hydrometer for measuring specific gravity, and various other objects made of different material – Kulagina nevertheless managed to get a compass apparently to zigzag across the table and the hydrometer to sail unaided across its basin of saline solution.

As with Home, no one ever managed to show that she was a fraud, and Kulagina successfully sued a Soviet journal which claimed she was. Sadly, she died in 1990, before being able to enjoy the freedom and celebrity that exposure in the West would, had she wanted it, undoubtedly have brought her.

Kulagina is not the only psychic to have given Communist scientists food for thought. China has its own psychic superstar in the form of a remarkable young man known to the Chinese press as 'Z'. By contrast with Kulagina, Z (whose name is Zang Baozheng), lives a life of privilege and luxury as 'resident psychic' at the Institute of Space-Medical Engineering (ISME) in Beijing, where Exceptional Functions of the Human Body (EFHB) research is carried out. This is essentially a military establishment that tends to keep its activities secret from the rest of the world, but research into Z before his arrival there in 1984 has been made available to the West.

Z's special *tour de force* is to apparently remove objects from sealed boxes by psychokinetic power alone. The tests devised by Chinese researchers to verify this improbable ability were simplicity itself, and rested on three basic principles: it should be impossible to open the containers without leaving evidence of having done so; the objects inside the containers should be impossible to duplicate; observation of the entire process should be uninterrupted, and take place from a variety of different angles. None of these safeguards put Z off his stride at all. Though it usually took him around five minutes to do so, it's claimed he could spirit things out of their containers at will. He apparently even managed psychokinetically to remove a live (and no doubt very perplexed) beetle from inside a tube.

The experiments devised to try to identify how he achieved his results became more ingenious. In one, several pieces of paper, which had been uniquely marked and treated with a chemical, were placed in one end of a glass container with a bottleneck in the middle. The other end of the container, nearer the opening, was stuffed with cotton wool treated with a chemical that would react on contact with the chemical used on the pieces of paper. The container was then irreversibly sealed. When Z had finished his work, the papers were lying beside the test tube. It's claimed traces of the chemical reaction showed that the papers must have somehow penetrated the cotton wool on their way out of the container, but the seal remained unbroken.

The only evidence of their work that ISME has released consists of frames from a high-speed film of Z extracting a pill from the bottom of a glass container. Not much is known about this particular experiment, but the photographs are interesting because they capture what some believe to be the actual moment of exit, which happens too rapidly for the human eye to witness.

There are other reports of PK research activity in China. One from the *Beijing Evening News* claimed that two girls from Hunan province had the ability to snap branches on trees and make buds come into bloom.

Of course the West has its own psychic superstar, in the shape of one of the most controversial figures ever to enter the paranormal scene: Uri Geller.

In a sense, Geller's career has both reflected and shaped the opinions held by the public and the media about psychic phenomena of all kinds. When his ability to bend metal, mend clocks and watches apparently with his mind alone, scramble computer disks, and a host of other psychokinetic activities were first made known in the early 1970s, the public lapped it up. Metal-bending parties were all the rage, research funds for departments interested in studying PK suddenly became available: the whole world was interested. That, of course, placed new pressures on Geller, and put new temptations in the way of his entourage. Pretty soon, some were being well paid for saying Geller was an illusionist; and others, perhaps in the belief that it would prolong his celebrity status, began to claim that his powers were ultimately controlled by an alien being visiting Earth in a spaceship (a story from which Geller distanced himself). For some years he was pursued by the sceptic James Randi, who claimed to be able to duplicate any 'trick' that Geller cared to attempt. When Geller's stock was low because of a public tirade by Randi, or a wild allegation by someone who knew him (or claimed to know him – 'news' journalists tend not to be fussy), so too parapsychology was considered silly and childish, and research funds began to dry up. For the whole of the 1970s, the fate and fortunes of Uri Geller and of the world of parapsychology were inextricably linked.

It is not my intention to retell Uri's story here – it has been covered plenty of times already. But there are some points worth making about the controversy that has always dogged the charismatic Israeli. I do not know whether Uri has real psychic abilities or not. However, since the seventies he has had another highly successful career identifying seams of precious metals, stones and oil, it's claimed, through his psychic ability.

Second, despite the widely held misconception that Geller runs a mile whenever the words 'laboratory tests' are mentioned, the truth is that he has submitted himself to more than a dozen series of tests under laboratory conditions and with both skilled research scientists and magicians present – for example, at the Stanford Research Institute, then under the supervision of British mathematician Professor John Taylor, and at Birkbeck College in London under Professor John Hasted. Each time he has 'passed' the tests handsomely. Debunkers have since picked holes in the methods used, but it is understandable if Geller feels reluctant to undergo a new battery of tests every time someone decides the last lot were flawed. Unless there is such a thing as a perfect experiment, this process could go on for ever.

Third, consider the classic line taken by Randi and others who like to debunk Geller and all he stands for: Geller is a magician, they say; anything he can do, I can do as well, or better. My response to this is threefold.

First, it is absolutely crucial for anyone involved in paranormal research of any kind to be aware of the possibility that what they are witnessing is a trick or an illusion. There is plenty of money to be made out of performing apparently paranormal activities in public, and many cheats and frauds have operated on the paranormal circuit for years. Of course, in some cases the fraud does not really deserve that name: a music hall audience watching somebody communicating with 'spirits' who happen to have a good line in comic repartee is doubtless colluding in a cosy illusion for the entertainment of all. But it is certainly wise to be aware of the possibility at all times: parapsychologists should *always* be sceptics.

But my second point is this: of course researchers are aware of the possibility of fraud. That is precisely what all the paraphernalia of the test laboratory is designed to rule out. That is precisely why academics design methodologies with such painstaking care, and have independent witnesses present as often as is practicable to confirm what they have seen. Behind the cry of fraud sometimes seems to be an assumption that research scientists carry out their work by sitting with their mouths wide open in wonder as an assortment of magicians and illusionists tramp through their labs performing a few hand-me-down tricks before taking their leave in a puff of smoke. Not so! Many scientists take the rigours of their profession very seriously, not least because their research grants are likely to disappear for good if they allow themselves to be fooled. Besides which, it is one thing for a skilled magician to put on a seamless show in a pre-prepared environment with all his props to hand, but quite another to walk into an unfamiliar lab with nothing and perform the same feats before a bunch of sceptical parapsychologists.

Let's not forget, too, that magicians and illusionists, often the most vocal critics of the paranormal, have a vested interest in trumpeting their own skills to the rooftops. In a competitive and demanding profession, they are unlikely to look favourably on someone who can apparently upstage them without even applying to join the Magic Circle, let alone learning how to pull a rabbit from a hat, or make a poodle out of balloons.

My third point is that the accusation of fraud is, by its very nature, impossible to refute. If Uri Geller is accused of being an illusionist and agrees to be tested, and those tests appear to rule out the possibility of trickery, then the response has frequently been: 'He must be an even better illusionist than we thought!' It is always open to debunkers to look at the conditions of the experiment and devise ways in which the research team could be fooled; but very often these boil down to one rather feeble suggestion along these lines: the research team is distracted for a moment, and while their backs are turned the trickster bends the spoon with brute force or swaps the real spoon for a bent one. Of course, no experiment is totally infallible, and at some point we have to make a judgement and say that we believe the results of such and such an experiment to be true because the sequence of events needed to perpetrate a fraud are far more absurd and unlikely than the results themselves.

In the second series of the programme we showed just how convincing the deceptions of such a man as French 'psychic' Jean-Pierre Girard can be when we caught him using micro-filament threads to drag objects off the table, completely hoodwinking the observer who was watching him at the time. But as much as it is important to bear in mind the possibility of fraud, it is just as important to recognize that just because something *can* be faked, that does not mean it *has* been faked.

As far as the credibility of psychokinesis is concerned, it really doesn't matter whether Uri Geller is a psychic or an illusionist or both; the evidence amassed from around the world is overwhelming anyway. In the specific skill of metal-bending, there are a number of people who can perform remarkable feats, whose work has been rigorously tested, but who have avoided the fog of publicity that surrounds Geller.

Professor John Hasted has conducted a long series of

experiments that seemed to provide irrefutable evidence that this particular branch of PK is genuine. Hasted often worked with children, and he varied his experiments frequently – partly in order to keep them interested, and to try to glean some information about the PK effect, rather than simply demonstrating that it existed. One of his experiments involved attaching 'strain detectors' to various pieces of metal distributed in different parts of the room. These measuring devices would record any strain taking place in the metal, and Hasted wanted to see whether he could get synchronous signals from more than one device at once. If so, he reasoned, this synchronicity could only be achieved by some sort of mechanical contraption linking the metal strips, which would be difficult to set up and very obvious, or by a genuine paranormal effect. Hasted successfully recorded synchronous signals from several detectors at once.

Hasted was also interested in 'impossible' PK effects. For one experiment he asked a subject to bend a rod made of a brittle alloy that is normally impossible to bend – it simply snaps instead. The only way to induce a bend is to apply light pressure over a long period. Nevertheless, the subject managed to bend the rod without snapping it, and well within the time that it would have taken to bend the rod by normal means. Like anyone who has studied metal-bending, Hasted was also intrigued by the widely observed 'plastic deformation' apparent during metal-bending. Frequently the metal becomes as soft as chewing gum under psychokinetic assault, and this is difficult to reproduce. A corrosive chemical might have the same effect, but not only would it by definition be very difficult to handle, it would also discolour the metal and cause the object to lose weight. Neither of these changes happened while Hasted was studying the phenomenon.

So much metal-bending has been observed by so many people that it is hard to believe it is not a genuine PK effect. To say otherwise suggests a mass conspiracy among parapsychologists and their subjects of a most bizarre kind, and the employment techniques that have never been satisfactorily identified or explained by those who would have us believe that the whole field is nonsensical. Unfortunately, lack of basic under-standing of how PK works makes it very difficult to design scientifically revealing tests.

The 'father' of micro-PK (the study of small-scale PK effects) is a man named Helmut Schmidt (not the former German chancellor!), who was the first to develop sophisticated methods of measuring PK in the laboratory, and is widely admired for the great elegance of the experiments and machinery he devised. The question that parapsychologists want answered today: is it possible for a subject to have a statistically significant effect on a random system? That system could be anything from the roll of a dice to the output of a computerized random number generator (RNG): it doesn't matter as long as it is truly random, and capable of having a pattern imposed on it from outside.

Schmidt's first device used as its source the random process of decay that occurs naturally in the Strontium-90 isotope. When the isotope emits an electron, a counter that is cycling through a series of, for instance, four states stops, and that state is registered to the user in the form of one of four light bulbs lighting up. The user can either register a prediction about which bulb will light up (a test for precognition), or attempt to influence the process by 'persuading' one bulb to light up more than 25 per cent of the time (a test for psychokinesis). In either case, the results are recorded automatically – in the early days on punched paper tape, but later on computer disk. This device had the advantage of being to all intents and purposes proof against cheating, and also capable of yielding data that could be subjected to statistical analysis.

His first two experiments tested for precognition, and showed incredible results. The probability of the ratio of registered hits to misses occurring by chance was less than one in 100 million – and this was over a series of 40,000 guesses. Schmidt checked his machine for bias or patterning but could find none. The first truly scientific PK experiment seemed to have been an extraordinary success. Schmidt tried a different approach, this time programming the machine to spool through a series of 15,000 targets, which were recorded, then replayed to the subjects. This time, rather than testing for precognition, Schmidt was hoping to find out whether his subjects could clairvoyantly read a predetermined sequence. Again the results were striking, with odds against chance of around a quarter of a million to one.

Schmidt now adapted his machine to provide what he thought would be a better test for PK. He reduced the number of states from four to two. However, the display consisted of a circular arrangement of nine light bulbs, with one illuminated. If an electron was emitted while the machine was in one state, the lighted bulb would move one place in one direction, and vice versa. Subjects simply had to try to influence the direction the light would take. But this time his subjects scored significantly *below* chance – an effect called 'psi missing' in which the results show an effect, but the reverse effect to that intended by the subject.

Schmidt continues to devise different ways of using his machines to test for different psychic abilities, all the while carrying out rigorous checks to ensure that what he is recording is not some internal flaw in his machinery that he has overlooked. So far, so good. No matter how many eminent sceptics inspect his work, none can find serious fault with it. One critic did suggest that the table on which the machine sat could have been sawn in half and the machine tampered with from below, but on this occasion it was the critic who was not taken seriously. Currently, Schmidt is working on a methodology that will effectively allow his peers and his critics to control the experiments. His work remains exemplary by any standards and for any field of science. And the best may be yet to come.

The balls thrown up in the air by Schmidt have been enthusiastically fielded by the team at the Princeton Engineering Anomalies (PEAR) project, which is headed by another great researcher in the field, Robert Jahn. Their approach is to amass data, and lots of it. Two of their devices, the random mechanical cascade (RMC) and the image scrambler, featured on the programme. With the first, we saw 9,000 ping-pong balls cascade down a peg-ball arrangement, sorting themselves into an unpredictable order. Could a human consciousness intervene to impose some kind of order on this chaos? So far, the results from PEAR confirm the pioneering work carried out by Schmidt – but now we are talking about databases containing not thousands, but millions of results, all based on a limited number of experiments carried out according to strict rules.

PEAR diverges from the approach taken by Schmidt in certain ways. They hope to be able to use the data to analyse whether individuals have identifiably unique effects on complex devices like the RMC, where the range of possible 'signatures' is immense. On the other hand they do not follow Schmidt's practice of trying to select individuals with above-average psychic abilities, believing that what they are witnessing is not so much the emergence of occasional 'psychic superheroes', but evidence of a range of abilities such as would be expected when studying any area of human endeavour. This open approach explains why their results are less dramatic. However, they remain significant – with odds against chance over the programme of between 5,000 and 10,000 to one – and, above all, consistent. The PEAR progress reports are certainly hard to refute, and very little is heard these days from the once vocal unbelievers.

Robert Jahn's insight into the nature of his work is, by contrast with the intellectual rigours of the theoretical physics that underlies micro-PK, comfortingly human:

The effects we are seeing in a controlled, laboratory-experimental environment are very similar to those which have been presumed over the ages. We are looking at the influence of the wishes and desires of the human operator on the performance of a physical process. Isn't that what we do when we hope for something? Isn't that what prayer is sometimes about? There are many common examples of a human tendency to try to impose desires on the way physical experience unfolds: what we do is look at this in the laboratory.

In the light of such insights, what can we say about the success of our viewers in influencing the outcome of the National Lottery? We asked Dean Radin of the University of Nevada what he thought:

We know from many years of experiments that if you have one person looking at a random system and you give them the instruction to affect that random system that they can do so to a small degree. So the question then is, what happens when you get lots of people all trying to put their attention on a random system? It wouldn't be surprising, given what we already know occurs in the lab, that a lot of people may be able to force certain numbers to come up that might otherwise not have come up . . . We don't really understand how that can happen, but we know that it happens.

Dean Radin has done some fascinating work on psychokinesis as an effect exercise by not just one person, but by a mass of people. He set an electronic random number generator to run continuously and monitored its progress. In particular, he noted the times of highly significant events that millions of people would have witnessed or been aware of through TV or radio, such as the giving out of the verdict in the O.J. Simpson trial, or the announcement of Oscar winners at the Academy Awards ceremony. Radin predicted that such events would cause an alteration in the random number generation – and he was right. Take the O.J. Simpson trial. The TV broadcast in which the verdict would be given out was scheduled to begin at 9.00 a.m. At precisely that time, each of the five random number generators that Radin had set up in different labs around the country registered an unexpected degree of order: that is to say, they changed from throwing out sequences of numbers that were truly random, to sequences of numbers that showed a distinct pattern. The odds against such patterns occurring at random would be around 300 to one. The same phenomenon occurred at 10.00 a.m., when the verdict was actually read out, except that this time the degree of order was 500 to one against. When you consider that these anomalies occurred *precisely* at the expected time in all five random number generators . . . The odds against that happening are more or less impossible to calculate definitely, but would be of the order of millions to one.

What does Dean Radin believe we are witnessing here? He theorizes that the history of PK research, and of his own studies into the effects of mass consciousness, all point to the conclusion that mind (as represented in his experiments by the effects of a mass change in consciousness) and matter (as represented by the physical machinery that generates random numbers) are essentially indivisible – rather in the way that atomic theory has demonstrated that matter and energy are indivisible. As an analogy, consider the different states that water can take: as steam it is a gas, as water it is a liquid, and as ice it is a solid. We know that the substance is essentially the same, even though it appears to be different in each case.

Mass consciousness effects are difficult to study, but Dean Radin speculates that during times when human consciousness is coherent – for instance, because millions of people are watching an international sporting event – then we would expect changes in matter to correspond with this coherence of consciousness. Mechanisms prone to disorder – a car that breaks down, a light that flickers on and off – might be less prone to play up. And if this power could be harnessed, extraordinary achievements would be possible. Perhaps we could mend the hole in the ozone layer, or lower the crime rate in some of our most deprived inner cities.

I will end this chapter with a description of another experiment carried out by the amazing Helmut Schmidt – one that produced what must surely rank as the most mysterious set of results in the history of parapsychological research.

Schmidt programmed one of his machines to generate a random series of binary (two-state) 'events', which he recorded, but which no one actually observed or attempted to influence or predict in any way. A day or so later this series was played back to subjects through headphones as a set of clicks distributed to the right and left channels, and they were simply asked to try to use psychokinetic power to weight the distribution of clicks in favour of one channel over the other. A significant psychokinetic effect was recorded.

Put simply, the subjects in this experiment were successfully influencing the outcome of a series of random events *that had already been generated*!

The same effect has been duplicated in several subsequent experiments, and now forms the basis for Schmidt's current research. We are stuck with this topsy-turvy phenomenon and had better try to understand what it means.

There *is* a tentative explanation for what is occurring here, though to follow it we have to dip a toe gingerly into the dark waters of quantum physics. Schmidt's experiments are, in fact, deeply bound up with the challenges physicists face in coming to terms with the new understandings about the behaviour of the universe at the micro, or subatomic level. For the machines he devised act in a decidedly quantum way: the events they generate are random and unpredictable, yet when run as an observed series of events they also conform exactly to statistical probability. The 'freezing' of their activity, which takes place when an electron is emitted and one of the states is displayed, is representative of the interaction between two worlds: the fixed, mechanical, Newtonian world we know and love, and the fuzzy, stateless world of quantum theory we are just beginning to come to terms with.

As described at the start of this chapter, a principle central to quantum theory is that the observer affects the observed, and this principle is directly tested when Schmidt's observers try to alter the outcome of the random event generating machines. In order to make sense of the baffling 'time-displaced' experiments described above, though, we have to take the idea to its logical conclusion and say that in fact the recorded random number session was not 'fixed' at all until it was observed – in this case listened to – by a subject. Until that moment, all of the possible outcomes of the original generation program remain possible. After observation, one has been chosen, with human consciousness taking the active role in the process that quantum theory would predict.

That sounds ridiculous. How could a tape with holes punched in it possibly not be fixed from the moment the holes are punched? And yet another remarkable experiment suggests that the ridiculous may prove to be true. Schmidt ran the time-displacement test consecutively with two different subjects, one known to have strong psychic abilities, the other known to have none. When the series was passed before the 'psychic' subject first, the results were significantly affected; but when the 'non-psychic' subject was the first to carry out the test, the results recorded by the 'psychic' subject showed no significant deviation from probability. It very much looked as if the 'non-psychic' subject had fixed the outcome of the series, leaving the 'psychic' no latitude for producing PK effects.

It is one of life's agreeable ironies that the least respectable area of scientific research – the paranormal – should find itself sharing lab-space, as it were, with one of the most prestigious and well funded of all – quantum physics, for that is what now seems to have occurred. In grappling with the question of how the observational consciousness of the human mind can fix and measure subatomic particles that are known to be entirely stateless, physicists are addressing exactly the same question as micro-PK researchers. Helmut Schmidt has even demonstrated how some of the least plausible implications of quantum theory might work out in practice. And when considering the interconnectedness of all things at the subatomic level, such that the act of observation fixes not just the thing observed but all things across time and space to which it is related, we even have an inkling of how it might be possible for psychics to read the past and future, to sense what they cannot see, or 'guess' what they cannot know.

We live in significant times.

6 Healing

I have told many stories in this book about people who have personal experience of paranormal phenomena, but one that was particularly inspiring was that of my own father. A few years ago he began to suffer from rheumatoid arthritis. This cripplingly painful disease, which affects so many people and so drastically alters the quality of their lives, has proved stubbornly resistant to the efforts of conventional Western medical experts to find a cure. The best most sufferers can hope for is to slow down the disease and alleviate its worst symptoms. Naturally I was distressed to learn that my own father was suffering from this affliction – the more so because the Dean of Rheumatology who was treating him at a major London hospital had told my father that the blood tests showed him to be about as badly affected as it was possible to be.

Once it was clear that the hospital could not offer much hope of improvement in his condition, I suggested to him that he visit a 'bio-energy healer' I knew, called Seka Nikoliz. She appeared in the first series of *The Paranormal World*, and of all the people I have met during the course of making both series, she remains one of the most impressive. My father was extremely sceptical that energy healing could do anything for him. However, as soon as I saw my father again shortly after he had seen Seka for a course of treatment, the effect was dramatic. 'That healer worked!' he declared. 'I feel fantastic.' It was obvious. Indeed, he looked younger, and his energy and optimism had returned. I asked him what the Dean of Rheumatology had said, and he replied that, although it defied explanation, the latest blood tests indicated that all traces of the illness had completely disappeared.

There are special problems and difficulties involved in talking about healing of any kind, psychic or spiritual healing in particular. To begin with, behind every attempt to heal there nearly always lies a history of suffering and pain, for – like my father – people usually go to healers who operate outside orthodox medicine only when all else has failed, when their own doctors have told them that there is nothing to be done except to grin and bear it. The emotional investment in healing is, therefore, very high: as much as people can be made joyful by a 'cure', they may be cast into despair by the lack of one. And if someone is miraculously 'cured' by a healer who is later exposed as a fraud, where does that leave the patient? Is their 'cure' fraudulent too?

Then there is the role of consciousness and willpower – something that is obviously very important when considering psychic healing, and perhaps spiritual and faith healing, too. Orthodox medicine is inclined to depersonalize the patient, to treat the sick person as an assembly of different mechanical parts, some in good working order, some not, and hence the idea of the patient contributing to the cure seems at best not worth wasting too much time over, at worst faintly absurd. As an example of this, you need only to consider how many conventional Western medical cures work by actually poisoning the affected area and destroying it. Healers, by contrast, nearly always talk in terms of *enabling* the cure rather than delivering it, of unblocking whatever it was that prevented the patient's own curative powers from swinging into action. The attitude of the patient must play a part here. Unless you have been there, it is almost impossible to guess what attitude or state of mind a chronically sick patient might be in when coming face to face with the real possibility of getting well, by whatever means: miracle cure, miracle drug or act of miraculous healing. Who would not, in such circumstances, make the superhuman effort of a lifetime to get better?

Faith in the cure seems to have a vital role in healing of all kinds – and this observation is not limited to alternative medical methods. For years, orthodox medical practitioners have been aware of the 'placebo effect', by which a drug known to have no physiological effect whatsoever can nevertheless have a beneficial effect on the patient to whom it has been administered.

Each time a new drug is tested, a placebo is used. Half the patients in a study are given the drug itself, the other half are given an alternative that is not expected to have any effect – a placebo. By this method, doctors can measure the effect of the drug against a 'control' group, whose members will show what would have happened if the affliction had been allowed to follow its normal course. Because of this method of testing, we have a vast amount of information about placebos and their effects.

Medical men have been aware of the phenomenon for many years, but in recent history it has mainly been regarded as a source of irritation. If every time a drug is tested the placebo effect comes into play, then the drug looks less effective than its proponents reckon it should. And indeed, to its discredit, the reaction of orthodox medicine to placebos has generally been dismissive. How can people be so gullible? has been the unspoken rebuke. But some have chosen to look more deeply into what is going on. In one study of 800 women who regularly took painkillers, different groups were given either a branded aspirin, a non-branded aspirin, a branded placebo, or a non-branded placebo. The aspirin worked better than the placebos. But what was remarkable was that the branded versions of both aspirin and placebo were markedly more effective than the non-branded versions. This experiment had been designed not to demonstrate the placebo effect, which was already well documented, but to try to measure it. The results suggested that the placebo effect – in this case, the branding – was responsible for around 30 per cent of the total improvement. Other studies, which have collated evidence from many different tests carried out across the world, have corroborated this approximate figure time and time again. A friend of mine wanted to bring out a range of tablets called Placebo, and for those really stubborn problems Placebo Plus! Is the placebo the most consistently effective 'drug' in medical history?

In another fascinating study, a group of fifty-six healthy students were told that they would be given either a pink or a blue pill. The pink one was a stimulant, the blue a sedative, and the students were told what symptoms to expect from each. In fact, all of them were placebos. But that is not to say they had no effect. All but three said they noticed a difference in how they felt. Over 65 per cent of the students who had taken blue pills said that they became less alert, and over 75 per cent said they felt drowsy. But only around 25 per cent of those who had taken a pink pill felt less alert, and under 35 per cent felt drowsy.

Sceptics will immediately object that these students were just doing as they were told; they knew what symptoms to expect, and so they dutifully recorded them. Fair enough, but how did they manage to invoke such physical symptoms as increased pulse and blood pressure? And why were there such consistently different reasons to different coloured pills that were otherwise identical? How can mere expectation (or gullibility, if you will) have such a strong, measurable effect, even – as other studies have shown – on very precise and concrete symptoms such as post-operative pain?

There are various theories as to what is going on. Some argue that the burst of confidence and new hope that the prospect of a cure can bring releases the body's own natural painkillers, called endorphins, into the bloodstream. Others say that it is the body's immune system that is stimulated by a positive mental attitude – just as prolonged stress can break down the immune system's ability to respond, so the relief from stress that the prospect of getting better brings may also strengthen it. Clearly there is much to be learnt about the physiological aspects of the placebo effect, and hopefully orthodox medicine will devote more resources to research in this area.

What we seem to be looking at here is an example of

human faith. In the case of the students, faith in what their teachers told them; in the case of the women who took part in the painkiller tests, faith in what marketing men had told them about the efficacy of brand names. Most often, though, it is faith in the doctor that triggers the placebo effect, and psychiatrist Michael Balint has noted that 'by far the most frequently used drug in general practice is *the doctor himself*'. This observation has also been borne out by tests indicating that the placebo effect works best when the placebo is administered by doctors who examine their patients carefully, express wholehearted enthusiasm for the placebo, and spend time with their patients while they are taking it. Such doctors inspire confidence in their patients, and so increase the efficacy of any cure they prescribe.

This very pronounced link between healing and faith is not new, of course. Healing has long been associated with religion, which is one of the strongest and most universal human expressions of the desire to believe in something, to have faith. Again, this is not an easy area to investigate. To some people, the very idea of investigating miracle cures or questioning Christian healers about what they do is blasphemous. On the other hand, if what healers do really works, and there is plenty of evidence to suggest that it does, then surely we should know how it operates so that everyone can benefit. How can that be achieved if healing has to remain a mystery?

The power of human faith is a difficult quality to measure and assess, and in some ways the placebo effect seems inadequate to explain all the forces at work when an act of healing takes place. What of the

135

healers themselves? Is their role limited to one of inspiring confidence and trust in the patient, or is there more? One remarkable experiment seems to suggest that there is. Dr Randolph Byrd, a cardiologist at San Francisco General Hospital and a devout Christian, programmed a computer to choose at random 400 patients who were to undergo cardiac surgery. He then asked prayer groups around the country to pray for the recovery of half of the patients after their operations and recorded the results. In 1985, at a meeting of the American Heart Association in Miami, Dr Byrd revealed that, to a statistically significant degree, the patients who had been prayed for were less prone to post-operative infection and pulmonary oedema (water on the lungs). The reaction of one notable sceptic and critic of alternative medicine was: 'If it works, it works.'

One of the most inspiring stories of healing through faith I have heard concerns Norman Cousins, who believed that we have within us a force or energy unknown to medical science with which, if we did but know how, we could heal ourselves. At the age of ten, Cousins was diagnosed as suffering from tuberculosis, the degenerative disease of the lungs, and was sent to a sanatorium. Cousins noticed that the optimistic, cheerful patients tended to get better, while the pessimists tended to get worse. Consciously aligning himself with the optimists, Cousins proved the point, recovered from the disease and led a full and rewarding life. Then, in 1979, he was told he was suffering from a rare form of paralysis which would certainly kill him within twelve months. Cousins promptly went to a hotel and prescribed himself a generous dosage of Marx Brothers movies. An unorthodox doctor also gave him large quantities of vitamin C. Cousins made a complete recovery – the first man in medical history to survive this disease. In 1983 Cousins suffered a myocardial infarction and congestive heart failure. In most cases people who suffer both simultaneously panic and die. Cousins did neither. Again he recovered, and subsequently took up a teaching career at UCLA medical school.

The psychobiologist Ernest Rossi tells of a shaman who pointed a 'death bone' at a South Sea islander. The victim believed in the curse, and despite the best efforts of doctors who did not believe that a man could be harmed in such a way, he died – possibly the victim of his own unshakeable faith in the efficacy of a shamanic curse. Nor is faith limited to religion: in 1957 the US Government reacted to the passionate representations of orthodox scientists and carried out an extraordinary attack on the work of Dr Wilhelm Reich. In a series of acts which, although they took place in 1957, were reminiscent of medieval witch-hunts or Stalinist purges, Reich's laboratory was destroyed by men wielding pickaxes, his books were burnt and he was thrown into prison, where he died shortly afterwards of a heart attack. Why? Because he had been experimenting and having some success with a device of his own invention called an orgone energy accumulator. Rather than face the possibility of a challenge to the articles of faith on which their own careers were founded, Reich's adversaries preferred to destroy him. The effectiveness – or otherwise – of his invention was not of the slightest interest to them. All that mattered was that the foundations of their own scientific beliefs should not be undermined.

Nearly all scientific innovators, whatever their field, have suffered from the entrenched attitudes of their opponents – though seldom to the extent endured by Reich (those interested in social history will note that this was also the period of the McCarthyite purges of anyone in public life who might conceivably be described as a communist).

Along with faith, another human emotional state that is often associated with healing is love: not love for a specific person, but a more general compassion, such as has been associated with great healers no matter how they choose to practise.

Rosemary Altea and Eddie Burks, as I described in Chapter 1, both believe they use the power of love to help release trapped or unhappy spirits. In telepathic research, it has been observed that couples who have a close, loving relationship are more likely to display a telepathic link than two people chosen at random. And if we extend the meaning of love to embrace the idea that there exists in any organized culture or society a bond of shared or fellow feeling that is primarily emotional in character and expresses itself as altruism or a desire to serve the common good, then we are coming close to Rupert Sheldrake's theory that was introduced in Chapter 4 on telepathy: that communication without any physical medium and across time and space may be accounted for by the presence of morphic fields.

Are these fields, too, animated and maintained by something we might call love – something with the power to bind together, integrate, make whole, and therefore heal?

The story of Christian spiritual healing from Jesus

onwards suggests that powerful psychic (and probably psychokinetic, since so many healers can work at a distance) forces are at work.

Malcolm Beasant works by the laying on of hands because he believes that vital energy can flow from one body to another and the patient receives a revitalizing charge that aids their recovery. Malcolm Beasant says that while working, 'I usually feel a tingling in my hands. Very often my entire body gets very hot. But it seems to be concentrated in my hands . . . It seems that I am able to focus and direct a pulse of my energy into another person. The person I am working on usually feels the heat from my hands, and very often a tingling like pins and needles all over their body.'

To rule out the possibility of a placebo effect, we gave Malcolm a patient who was unlikely to be susceptible to suggestion: Sasha, an Alsatian dog suffering from chronic arthritis, an ulcerative skin condition, acute eczema. These conditions were so painful that her owners had considered putting Sasha to sleep.

Malcolm treated Sasha for half an hour on three occasions. Her owners were astonished that she reacted so peacefully to his presence, remaining docile and calm throughout the treatment.

After the treatment, her owners reported a definite improvement in both skin conditions, and said that the arthritis was clearly less painful. But the most striking effect was psychological. From being lethargic and uninterested in life, Sasha became alert and happy again. In the words of one of her owners: 'I took her for a walk and she was a different dog – lively, running ahead of me, whereas before I'd been almost dragging her along. Her old interest had come back. I have to say that it was remarkable. But I can't explain it.'

England rugby international Ben Clarke was an altogether more challenging and sceptical patient for Malcolm Beasant, but he too was won over. Ben had been struggling with a recurrent hip injury that had been aggravating him for many months. He had received plenty of conventional treatment, but the problem kept coming back. He too had three half-hour sessions with Malcolm Beasant. 'It was a strange feeling. I felt some warmth there, and could feel a pulse around where he was working,' said Clarke. Interestingly, Malcolm worked not on his hip, but on his ankle, where he believed the problem originated. Ben Clarke confirmed this view. After the treatment, he was converted. 'The treatment,' he said, 'has achieved a remarkable improvement. I'm absolutely delighted. I wasn't sure about it before, I was very, very sceptical, but I'm certainly convinced of it now.'

It appears that Malcolm Beasant was able to home in on and begin to cure a condition that months and months of expensive and expert conventional treatment had failed to alleviate. I firmly believe that we should research the forces at work here. We spend a fortune every year developing new variations of drugs which are mildly more effective than the last ones, while the medical establishment still routinely dismisses types of healing that have proved their worth time and time again.

Orthodox medicine may in fact have worked its way into a corner, because it is rapidly becoming too expensive for even affluent societies to afford; the types of healing described above may offer a way out of that corner. I'm not saying that we should throw away all the knowledge we have painstakingly accumulated over the centuries, because the scientific approach taken over the last three centuries has served us well. It's just that throwing more and more money into the most expensive forms of medicine seems foolish right now; why not throw just a fraction of that money towards the cheaper alternatives?

Christianity is not the only religion in which healing holds a central place; many religions and cultures give it the same high status. The rituals may differ, but the essence of the practice remains the same: to invoke some therapeutic power – perhaps a universal life force that both healer and patient share, or a deity associated by the healer with that life force – and apply it to the sick. If to us this is a 'paranormal' phenomenon, in others it is an accepted part of the social and cultural circumstances in which they live. Some people tend to assume that such societies are somehow backward and benighted, and that the Western way of life is the one to which all others will gravitate. But anthropological studies have proved that in reality such 'primitive' societies are at least as ruthless as we are about expelling useless rituals and healing procedures from the mainstream, and are far more open to incorporating any new medical procedure which can be seen to work. In other words, to use the jargon of modern business, they may be more 'results-driven' than we are. One study by E. F. Torrey has shown that tribal witch-doctors actually have a much better record in treating mental illness than psychiatrists do.

In such societies, it is the figure of the shaman that is of most interest. The shaman – whether an Aboriginal 'clever man', a tribal witch-doctor or a Native American medicine man – appears to possess a rich assortment of skills, powers, know-how and techniques.

Shamanism properly refers to practices carried out in Siberia and Central Asia, but the term has been widened to include similar spirit-contacting procedures the world over. It has been described as 'the world's oldest profession', and there is evidence that shamans were active 20,000 years ago. In those days, they probably combined even more roles than they do now – telling or acting out stories that helped define or explain the world in which they lived, for instance, and perhaps acting as magicians and entertainers. Many shamans believe that the key to their functions lies in their ability to contact spirits by entering a 'trance' that acts as a gateway to the spirit world. Once there, the shaman apparently has access to information and powers that are not available in the ordinary world.

When it comes to healing, the shaman does not share the overriding interest of Western medicine in prolonging life. Rather, the shaman must guard the spirit of the living, ensure that it is not driven out by a traumatic event, disease, or threatened by some kind of hex, curse or malediction applied by an enemy. In Western terms the distinction between these two types of illness might be described as the difference between systemic or pervasive illnesses such as those characterized by whole body symptoms (fevers, sweats, diseases of the blood or nervous system, mental disorders) and invasive, localized symptoms (tumours, stones, local infections), although, of course, there is no precise relationship between the two.

If their affliction is diagnosed as systemic, loss of

contact with the spirit may be given as the cause, and the cure is for the shaman to enter the spirit world and lead the spirit back to the safety of its bodily host. If the affliction is invasive, then the shaman apparently sucks out the 'alien object' and banishes it for ever.

There is plenty of anecdotal evidence that shamanic cures are effective, but it is very difficult to judge whether the healing is psychic in nature. One clue may be that in both types of sickness, some kind of evidence is required to indicate to the patient that the cure has been effective. In the case of invasive sickness, a stone, a piece of bloody offal or a feather may be produced, shown to the grateful patient, then made to disappear. If soul-loss is the problem, then the shaman will tell the patient a story about the heroic struggle he undertook, the evil spirits he slew and the dreadful trials he had to undergo in order to lead the spirit to safety – a bloodied weapon may be shown as evidence that the drama took place.

This is not so very different from the methods employed by Gerald di Padua, the star of Brazilian spiritual healing who featured in the healing programme. I personally believe that generally 'psychic surgery' is nothing more than trickery and any positive effects upon the patient are purely placebo. However, I do not claim to know whether di Padua's brand of psychic surgery is real or fake, but either way the need to convince the patient of the cure is the same. In this respect, di Padua's reputation is clearly of great value – in the queues that form outside his clinic, there is much discussion of his abilities and the wonderful cures he has effected. So, too, the discussions at the bedside, the cups apparently containing 'ectoplasm' and 'spiritual medicines', and, of course, the summoning of the spirits themselves, all help add to the idea of a significant event taking place under the aegis of powerful forces.

In the West such activities have been described as nothing more than sleight of hand and trickery. The important thing is for the patient to have faith in the cure, and it is part of the shaman's job to inspire that faith. Again, Western medics would call this a placebo effect, although no Western practice that I know of activates the effect with such sophistication. There are also obvious parallels with the quantum idea that a cure is a cure if the patient thinks it is one, and with the notion that the healer's primary function is to facilitate recovery by activating the patient's own recuperative energies.

Some research into the activities of African shamans, called *sangoma*, gives further insights into the psychic elements in their activities. Adrian Boshier, an Englishman, studied the *sangoma* and eventually became one himself. He noted that during the training process, at the hands of a teacher called a *baba*, initiates had to carry out exercises in clairvoyance: the *baba* would hide an object, then require the trainee *sangoma* to go and find it. Later in the training, the commands appear to be given telepathically. Certainly finding lost objects is a routine task required of any fully trained *sangoma*, and Boshier is convinced that the skill is essentially psychic.

Whether psychic or not, the actual focus of all *sangoma* activity is on the spirits of ancestors who play such a key role in African life. They believe that if someone is ill, it is up to the *sangoma* to contact the spirit and act as a medium for the advice that spirit will give. Depending on the nature of that advice, the application of herbal medicines may follow, or some kind of ritual – dancing, singing, chanting – may be prescribed. This is gentle stuff compared with parallel practices in other cultures, where the business of making contact with the spirit world is much more dramatic. The process may begin with periods of fasting and sexual abstinence. In Native American cultures, this may be followed by a 'sweat bath', which is something like a very long and very hot sauna; the shaman may also concentrate on specific images, or stare into flames, or isolate himself from human contact and sit in darkness. The build-up to the climactic moment when the shaman believes he enters the spirit world may involve the whole village in chanting, drumming and dancing, and sometimes psychedelic drugs are administered. In societies where the rituals associated with shamanism are extensive – in Java and the Philippines, for example – the process may be very hard on the shaman, who will need some time to recover from his spiritual journey.

For all that I would love to see it properly investigated by science, I will admit that the kind of spiritual healing so far described is very hard to analyse. In the case of spiritual healers, is it really the case that the spirits or deities to whom the healers appeal are working the miraculous cure? Or is it the power of auto-suggestion, the power of the patient's own belief in the cure, that does the trick? Or is there a psychokinetic effect, as discussed in the previous chapter, by which healers actually have a physical effect on the bodies of their patients, shrinking tumours to nothing? There are no ready answers to these questions. Religious or spiritual healers tend to be wary of the laboratory. Many are perfectly happy to do demonstrations but do not like to have them reduced to their component parts and tested until some repeatable phenomenon is observed – the standard scientific methodology. However, some revealing experiments have been carried out.

One of the first was devised by Professor Bernard Grad at McGill University in the USA. He divided a number of mice into two groups, and under anaesthetic removed a small patch of skin from each of their backs. In one group, the wounds were allowed to heal naturally. But the others were put under the care of a healer called Oskar Estabany. Since it is known anyway that mice will heal more quickly if stroked and held in human hands (the precise physiological reasons have not been identified), Estabany was allowed only to touch the cages in which his mice were held. Nevertheless, his group healed significantly faster than the control group.

Grad then set up an experiment with plants. Again, two groups were set up – one group of plants was grown in a chemical solution known to be favourable to growth, while the other group was grown in salt water – a decidedly hostile environment for most plant life. The first group of plants was watered in the normal way, but the second group was given water from a jug that Estabany had held in his hands. Despite the obstacle they faced of starting life in salt water, the group tended by Estabany grew significantly better than the control.

William Braud of the Mind Sciences Foundation in

Texas has taken such research a little further. He aimed to find out whether it was possible for the power of the mind to be used to exert a calming influence over a subject and devised an experiment to test this. Thirty-two individuals were divided into two groups – one diagnosed as suffering from stress-related problems, the other as being generally free of stress. Each in turn was linked to a polygraph, while the 'influencer' went to another room and tried to relax the subject by what Braud described as 'distant mental influence'. The influencers followed instructions on a pack of cards – sealed until the test began – which ordered them either to do nothing or to exert a calming influence for a given space of time. By linking those periods with the polygraph printouts, an accurate record of the effect of the influencers was obtained.

The results here were mixed. Of a total of thirteen separate series of tests with 271 different subjects, based on the above idea but with a number of variations, the results of all showed that the influencers had some effect, and in six that the effect was considered significant. With the subjects who suffered from stress, the influencers had considerable success, but no notice-able change was recorded in those who did not. Overall, the odds against the results occurring spontaneously were 43,000 to one – and this in a study where only a handful of the influencers had a history of healing ability.

Another of Braud's studies is perhaps the most striking of all attempts to define the relationship between healing and PK. Braud drew blood from volunteers and placed it in a test tube with saline solution, which causes the gradual destruction of the blood cells. The volunteers were then asked to try to delay the deterioration by thought alone – and this they succeeded in doing to a remarkable degree (the odds against this happening by chance are almost 200,000 to one). But the most notable finding was that people were only able significantly to delay the destruction of *their own blood*. Once again, this result resonates with Sheldrake's theory of morphic fields. Is there a bond between blood and its human source even after the two have been separated, a bond that is like a low-level morphic field operating within the more complex fields represented by human, animal and insect societies?

One final study is worth mentioning. In 1996 researchers at the University of Nevada decided to try to test the hypothesis that a voodoo healing ritual could have a remote calming effect on a patient. In the tests the patient was asked to create a doll in his or her own likeness, and provide the healer with personal belongings, pictures and an autobiographical sketch. Healer and patient were then separated, and the healer was asked to exert a calming influence on the patient. Using the dolls and personal effects as a focus for traditional voodoo magic, the healers were able to alter blood volume and heart rate significantly in their subjects – this effect was demonstrated consistently throughout the study. It was not the intention of the researchers to explain what was happening; but I believe they show beyond reasonable doubt that the phenomenon of remote healing really does exist.

Research into unorthodox medicine is not very far advanced on the whole, and as a result this chapter has probably raised many more questions than it has answered. But that is as it should be. As systems of medicine proliferate, caution is essential. Health is such a complex, highly charged issue that one cannot simply welcome every new idea or approach with open arms and give its practitioners *carte blanche* to do whatever they please.

On the other hand, a little bit of openness is needed, and a willingness to recognize that the spirit of radical inquiry is what inspires and enables real improvements to be made to any system, however advanced. Osteopathy now does as much as any branch of medicine to keep those people mobile who would once have had to take to their beds – not to mention the benefits it has delivered in terms of releasing thousands of people from debilitating back pains. And yet less than twenty years ago, the very mention of the word 'osteopath' may well have had your GP tut-tutting over the prescription pad, warning you of the dangers of putting yourself in the hands of amateurs, before prescribing a fortnight off work.

Orthodox medicine has achieved great things, prolonging life, improving its quality, and banishing some of the diseases that have scourged the world. However, the problems we will face in the future will certainly differ from those we have faced in the past, and we will need a new approach to deal with them. Besides which, as I've already stated, orthodox medicine has become so expensive that we also need alternatives.

I don't pretend to know which alternatives will offer the best way forward, but I do know that there are plenty of avenues open that are well worth following. It's worth remembering that all of the healers I've described here have been dealing not with simple, straightforward patients who will as often as not get better by themselves, but with the rejects and no-hopers, the ones who followed the established route but were told in the end that there was nothing that could be done for them. Given this simple fact, I think their success is often astonishing, and deserving of our deepest admiration.

7 Superhumans

In 1991, eleven-year-old Elizabeth Dawson displayed 'superhuman' strength when she lifted a twelve-stone trailer with one hand to save her eight-year-old sister who was trapped beneath it.[1]

One of the themes of this book has been that there is no great gulf between paranormal phenomena and ordinary people. I'm willing to bet that most people reading this will have experienced some kind of 'psychic' event at some time in their lives – perhaps without really thinking there was anything unusual going on.

The realm of the unexplained is vast, unimaginably much larger than the realm of knowledge. In different ways, it touches us all at some time in our lives.

To finish with, I want to look at people who are clearly exceptional, but who probably wouldn't claim to have psychic powers. What they do have is the ability to make their bodies do what most people's the bodies would instinctively refuse to do. Mostly through hard work, exercise, meditation and concentration they have developed levels of physical and mental control that are quite simply superhuman. Their abilities certainly look paranormal: and yet in many cases those 'paranormal' abilities represent an

1 *Today* newspaper, 4 September 1992.

achievement of which, in theory at least, anyone is capable.

Having said that, let me repeat what I said several times during the TV show on the subject: *Do not attempt any of the feats described below or seen on television yourself!* Nearly all of them are potentially fatal, and if they can be learned at all it is only after years of training and exercise.

Man or Superman?

I will start with Valeri Lavrinenko, the man who performed some of the most remarkable feats of strength, control and endurance ever seen on television. Those who saw the show will no doubt remember it clearly. When you first see Lavrinenko, he looks ordinary enough. Obviously he is strong and very fit, but he does not have the body of one of the Gladiators. So if he has superhuman strength, that strength must primarily be in the mind.

That diagnosis is confirmed by the demonstration in which he was hooked up to an electrocardiograph machine (ECG) that measured his heartbeat and then, in front of a full studio audience and with a doctor present, Lavrinenko raised his heartbeat to well over 140 beats per minute. Dr Roberts commented that this is the sort of level you would expect to get if you took Linford Christie's pulse immediately after he had run the 100 metres. But that was not the end of it. He then began to lower his heart rate, doing it so fast that the ECG machine lost track and was trailing behind. When it finally caught up, Lavrinenko's heartbeat had fallen below faulty, and an alarm was triggered: if Lavrinenko had been under anaesthetic, immediate action would have been taken by the medical team attending him to bring his heart rate up again. Instead, Lavrinenko's heart rate went on going down, until it seemed to everyone present that it must have stopped altogether. Dr Roberts reckoned that at this point his heart was beating at around ten beats per minute and momentarily stopped. I can tell you that there were some very shocked faces in the audience that night! Of course it was to be expected that in the aftermath of the show there were some mutterings about this demonstration having been rigged. Undeterred, Lavrinenko came back in the second series and performed exactly the same feat, this time with sophisticated imaging monitors to register the event. The cardiologist we invited along as a witness declared himself perfectly satisfied that the demonstration was genuine.

Lavrinenko managed to survive the battering his body received at the hands of the high-voltage stungun we filmed him applying first to his arms and then to his neck. That gun delivers an 80,000-volt punch, yet he held it to his body while repeated pulses of electricity pummelled through him. The expert we had in the studio, who knows the capabilities of this particular weapon very well, was flabbergasted: 'Usually they go down like they've been poleaxed,' he said. 'They go into spasm or shake like they've had a fit or a heart attack. Frankly, I'm surprised to see him still standing.'

But the two most spectacular achievements in Lavrinenko's repertoire were yet to come. Many will have seen big men haul huge loads before: it is a common enough feat in strong-man competitions. But a forty-ton train is an exceptional load even by these standards, and, as already observed, Lavrinenko is not a particularly big man. The fact that such feats of strength are usually carried out by men twice his size may suggest that Lavrinenko is not relying on physical strength alone.

That impression was confirmed when he announced that he would pull the train using cables harnessed to steel wire loops passed through the muscles of his forearms. The medical staff present really were worried that the steel wire loops would simply slice through his forearms like a garrotte through cheese. Lavrinenko claimed that he could make the muscles of his forearms as hard as rock – but again the question is, how? Again the answer must be that some kind of mental ability is at the heart of this phenomenal display of strength and endurance.

The last demonstration he gave, when he frightened the life out of everyone present by staying under water for nearly seven minutes – is probably the most life-threatening, since the dangers of blacking out while under or while expending the energy needed to come to the surface are considerable. We know that the idea is to oxygenate the blood sufficiently to make breathing unnecessary, and that by hyperventilating in advance the blood can effectively be saturated with oxygen. However, there are limits – and six minutes is generally thought to be as much as the human body can achieve without suffering brain damage, even if the subject expends as little energy as possible while under (for instance by going into a trance as Lavrinenko appeared to do). So how did Lavrinenko manage to do without breathing for nearly seven minutes?

One possibility is that the capillaries in his lungs that oxygenate the blood are simply more efficient than most people's – either because he has practised so much they have developed or because he was born with them. We know that pearl divers in the South Pacific can also stay under water for many minutes – although whether this is a facility developed by genetics and evolution or by hard work is not known. Another possibility is suggested by the PK experiments carried out by William Braud and described in the previous chapter. Braud's subjects were able to influence the rate of decay of their own blood. Is Lavrinenko able to alter the composition of his own blood in some way, so that it can temporarily absorb more oxygen than usual? Or is he perhaps able to 'shut down' various organs psychokinetically so that their demand for blood is reduced to nil for the duration of the test?

Lavrinenko himself is not forthcoming about how he achieves these incredible feats: these demonstrations are how he makes his living, and it is perhaps not surprising that he wants to maintain the mystique of the superman that surrounds him.

The zone

They may not be in the Lavrinenko league, but professional sportsmen know that strange things can happen when you push yourself to the limits of endurance and enter 'the zone'.

The zone is a neuropsychological state that athletes claim they enter. They say they feel as if they have broken through a barrier and come out the other side feeling suddenly capable of putting in a new burst of speed, or lifting a heavier weight, or running a few miles further. The feeling is usually accompanied by a sensation of being superbly relaxed and co-ordinated, of easily being able to better any level of performance yet attained, and of time slowing down so that there is plenty of time to carry out difficult acts of co-ordination.

More complex and perhaps overwhelming sensations are also experienced: the feeling of clairaudiently knowing what an opposing team intends to do next, for instance; or an out-of-body experience in which the mind appears to detach itself and leave the body to run itself; or the feeling of having suddenly grown in size and strength, or dramatically improved in ability.

Entering the zone is usually a sublime experience for the athlete involved, and, needless to say, it can lead to vastly improved performances. A key quality of the experience is that anxiety about winning or losing, about whether a performance has been good or bad, about what will happen next – all such pressures drop away, leaving the mind focused, still and in harmony with the actions of the body.

Such qualities have long been a central objective of martial arts, as we shall see, but sports men and women in the West tend to have lagged behind in terms of mental preparation. Now, however, creating the right conditions for athletes to enter the zone has become a mainstay of sports psychology, and meditational and visualization techniques are widely used to encourage them to take a more holistic approach to sporting achievement.

Again, we are very close to talking about psychic powers here. If it is possible to use the powers of the mind to elevate sporting performance over and above what is possible in the ordinary course of events, then it must surely be possible to use those powers in other ways. And as previous chapters have shown, the evidence that such powers need not be limited to the confines of our bodies is mounting all the time.

Martial arts

Of course, Lavrinenko is not alone in performing acts that most would consider impossible, although he is certainly the most remarkable I have ever encountered. Traditions associated with overcoming the natural limitations of the human body by force of will can be found in the Indian subcontinent, where fakirs have been demonstrating their ability to rise above pain for many centuries. But first we will look at a different, less mystical tradition, which stresses its foundations in the abilities of the human body: the practice of martial arts.

Martial arts are very widely practised: as a form of self-defence, as exercise, as a kind of physical meditation, or simply as a discipline that can enhance the lives of its practitioners. It takes many different forms, some of which originate in China, some in Japan, others in Korea. All, however, share a belief that the basis of all physical skills is to understand and exploit the universal life force that flows through all of us, and which in martial arts is usually referred to as *chi*.

Chi is believed by some to be the force that animates and links all forms of energy, and as such it must embrace many opposites: physical and mental; male and female; active and passive; yin and yang. Our tendency is to define things by dividing them into their constituent parts, which does not make much sense

157

where *chi* is concerned: its very essence is apparently its indivisibility.

A typical exercise in the process of learning to understand and master *chi* will involve a series of formal bodily movements performed at a slow and regular pace while the mind is alert and focused, but also clear of distraction, relaxed and still. Breathing is vital to the process of accumulating *chi* and centring it just below the navel, which is where the natural centre of the body is held to be: students may be asked to visualize the hips as a bowl into which *chi* is poured – and from which it can easily be spilled if the balance and poise of the body or mind are upset.

The emphasis on the crucial part played by the state of mind of the practitioner derives from a simple observation: if blinded by anger, or paralysed by fear, or rendered impotent by stupidity, the most skilled fighter in the world will fall victim to an inferior opponent. Furthermore, control of *chi* is not, it is claimed, dependent on physical strength, but on harmonizing mental and physical energies. Some believe that mental discipline tends to increase with age, advantages lost with the passing of youth are more than compensated for by the clarity and wisdom of the older master: the greatest practitioners of martial arts are nearly always old men. Their muscles may have waned and their bones turned brittle, but because they are able to absorb and wield so much *chi*, they are immensely strong.

However, it is important to appreciate that the aim is to rise above both mental and physical levels, and to attain a state of oneness with the *chi*. When this state is achieved, winning or losing become unimportant: the sole aim is to harmonize with the *chi*, to remain in perfect balance with the flow of energy, and this specifically entails *not* thinking with the rational mind, nor acting independently with the body, for both are but single manifestations of the multifaceted higher force with which the fighter wishes to be one.

Someone who has spent many years exercising and learning about *chi*, it is said, will eventually achieve a clarity of vision that is very like a kind of focused clairvoyance: nothing can be hidden from the greatest martial arts masters, who are said to know that an attack is about to be launched before the attacker himself has conceived the idea. Apparently this awareness derives from developing oneness with the *chi*. Because the force is universal and shared, not divisible and individual, when two fighters engage, the *chi* that flows in and around them will be a single force, and therefore the combatant who has the greatest control of the *chi* will take control of the contest and ultimately win it because even his assailant's own resources will be at his command. Indeed, the types of martial arts that take the concept of *chi* to its logical conclusion hardly involve any attacking moves: all the energy expended by the opponent is simply and instantly turned against him.

By controlling and directing *chi*, astonishing actions would be possible. The classic demonstration, beloved by every Kung Fu film, is to smash through piles of wooden blocks, tiles or bricks with the hand, foot, elbow or even the head. The ability to withstand heavy blows and deep sword-cuts is also achieved by advanced practitioners; some even claim immunity from fire. In training, some advanced practitioners have been known to pound their hands into bowls full of stones heated over a fire in order to harden them. As we saw on the show the legendary founders of Kung Fu, the Shaolin monks, are able to perform extraordinary displays of strength and endurance by focusing *chi*. The Ninja, known for their skills as assassins, studied a form of martial art called Ninjitsu. Its followers were reputed to be able to dislocate and relocate their own limbs, to use meditational and breathing techniques to stay under water for long periods of time, and to control the rate at which their own hearts beat so as to enable them to hide in places close to their victims.

The great Japanese master of the martial art Jiu Jitsu, Morihei Ueshiba, was only five feet tall and weighed in at less than nine stone, but his control of *chi* was legendary. When he rooted himself to the ground, centring his *chi* and driving it downwards, he could resist the efforts of several large men to pick him up. By directing *chi* upwards he could make himself incredibly light – apparently his favoured method of demonstrating this was to walk across stepping stones of delicate china teacups. He would then ask his students to try, and exercised the humorous side of *chi* by watching them hop up and down in an attempt to avoid the piles of broken china beneath their feet. By directing *chi* outwards, he could send assailants flying through the air with the minimum of physical exertion.

Ueshiba went on to develop Aikido, which means 'The way of harmony with the spirit of the universe'. The stated aim of this beautiful martial art is the unification of mind, body and *chi* into a single whole, and the manifestation of love for all things in all actions. Again, it is believed that control of the *chi* that is available in a contest is the key to victory. The philosophy behind Aikido has a charming origin. Ueshiba was, it is said, sitting under a persimmon tree one day when the earth trembled and a spirit rose up from the ground. The spirit covered Ueshiba's body with a veil, then turned him golden and infused his mind and body with light. At that instant he understood the mind of God, and hence of all things, including the birds that chattered above him in the persimmon tree. His special insight was that the essence of a martial art should be God's love for all things, and that embracing and applying that love should be the central aim of Aikido.

Ueshiba claimed that his harmony with *chi* was such that he was able to dodge bullets, and the way he describes the feat is reminiscent of psychic phenomena. While on a trip to Mongolia in 1924, he was attacked by bandits armed with rifles. As the bullets sped towards him, Ueshiba claimed he sensed from which direction they were coming and then 'saw' them as little pebbles of brilliant white light that he was able to turn away from before they could strike him.

In all its many guises, the martial arts tradition overtly recognizes and exploits a power or force that is not acknowledged by science. To that extent, martial arts depend on the existence of paranormal phenomena. But many of its teachers and practitioners would not necessarily see it like that: to many *chi* is a very real force indeed. There is no onus on the ancient martial arts tradition to justify itself to the relatively new methods of science.

8 The Future

Reasonable men adapt themselves to the world. Unreasonable men adapt the world to themselves; that's why all progress depends upon unreasonable men.

George Bernard Shaw

Proponents of the Gaia theory have a beautiful metaphor with which to describe the Earth: they see it as a living organism, with the oceans as its blood, the rainforests its lungs, the days and nights its heartbeats. By the same token, couldn't we also describe human consciousness as the Earth's brain, or, as the brilliant author Peter Russell calls it, 'The Global Brain'? By the year 2000 there will be approximately the same number of communication connections on the Earth as there are neural pathways in the brain. Many others see the year 2012 as highly significant as it is the year that ends the current cycle of the Mayan calendar, and is predicated to be a turning point for humanity. Could this turning point take the form of a coming to consciousness of the brain of Gaia by way of the interconnectedness of all its billions of constituent parts?

Already this century the work of Niels Bohr and his successors has completely revolutionized our understanding of the way the universe operates, and offered us scientific theories for phenomena that seem to fly in the face of all reason – in some respects, the atomic events described by quantum physics now look much more paranormal than healing or telepathy. Meanwhile, it is estimated that 80 per cent of all information in the world has been generated since 1964. We are into an exponential curve of technological development. Most of the technologies we use daily have been invented only in the very recent past, and would have been considered absolutely inconceivable less than a century ago.

Imagine what people in 1899 expected of the next century and compare that with what has actually happened. Is there any reason to suppose that our current predictions for the future will also turn out to be wildly short of the mark? The butt of yesterday's ridicule may be the gateway to tomorrow's technology, and this has often been the case. From the persecution of Galileo to the accusation that Louis Pasteur was in league with the devil and the trashing of Wilhelm Reich's lab, the current upholders of orthodox science have always been tough on radical thought, acting at times like fundamentalists. Some degree of scepticism is healthy, of course; but so too is some degree of openness to new ideas and new possibilities, even if – or perhaps *especially* if – they seem not to conform to the current view of things. We need open-minded, benevolently sceptical scientists to investigate the paranormal, because they are the people best equipped to do so. Some phenomena only recently regarded as nonsense by the scientific establishment have now been proved beyond any reasonable doubt.

In a hundred years from now some of the things we currently assume to be true scientifically will be false, but science fiction will remain the same – forward-looking, often inadvertently predictive and, above all, creative.

Science doesn't have all the answers but perhaps it can provide us with better questions.

Sources of Further Information

Organizations are listed in alphabetical order within each category. The majority of those listed are national or umbrella groups who should be able to put you in touch with local services in your area. This list is for information only and is not intended as an endorsement.

General
The Association for the Scientific Study of Anomalous Phenomena
20 Paul Street
Frome
Somerset
BA11 1DX
The Society provides a register of acknowledged investigators and consultants who can offer help, information and advice. Also organize public meetings, lectures and exhibitions. Write to the above address regarding membership, which provides research benefits and free or reduced-cost publications.

Society for Psychical Research
49 Marloes Road
Kensington
London
W8 6LA

The purpose of the Society is to advance the understanding of events and abilities commonly described as 'psychic' or 'paranormal', without prejudice and in a scientific manner. Publishes a quarterly newsletter and journal, and offers a wide range of publications, lectures, study days, weekend workshops and an annual international conference (members are eligible for reduced rates). The Society's library is open to all members. Write to the above address for membership details.

RESEARCH LABORATORIES
The following laboratories carry out parapsychological research (scientific research into possible psychic phenomena). They may be able to provide information about research into the paranormal and occasionally require volunteers (who should live locally) to take part in research projects.

Edinburgh University – Psychology Department
7 George Square
Edinburgh EH8 9Z

(Information can also be found on the Internet, through 'University of Edinburgh', or 'Parapsychology')

University of Hertfordshire – Psychology Department
College Lane
Hatfield
Herts AL10 9AB

(Information can also be found on the Internet, through 'University of Hertfordshire' – Psychology page)

Health and Healing

Note: The Department of Health advice on complementary therapies is as follows: Before a person embarks on a form of treatment, they should satisfy themselves as best they can that the treatment offered is likely to be effective, or at least unlikely to cause harm; and that the practitioner is an established member of an established profession and carries proper insurance. They are further advised to seek the advice of their GP.

People seeking alternative or complementary therapies should be aware of the danger of untrained practitioners. There are some who practise without recognized qualifications. We recommend, therefore, that you check with either the British Complementary Medicine Association or the Institute for Complementary Medicine before choosing a practitioner, both are listed below. I have also included a list of other organizations that are associated with many of the subjects of this book. However, do *not* consider this an endorsement in any way whatsoever; it is only for reference.

British Complementary Medicine Association
39 Prestbury Road
Cheltenham
Gloucestershire
GL52 2PT
Tel: 01242 226770

This organization operates a Code of Conduct that is common to all member organizations. Telephone or write to the above address for guidance and the name and contact numbers of healers in your area.

Health Watch
Box CAHF
London
WC1N 3XX
Tel: 01483 503106

Health Watch is a registered charity whose members include doctors, lawyers, scientists and journalists. The association's aims include the promotion of high standards of health care and the development of good practices in the assessment and testing of treatments. To become a member and receive their newsletter and other literature, write to the membership secretary at the above address.

Institute for Complementary Medicine
PO Box 194
London SE16 1QZ
Tel: 0171 237 5165

Activities include a national registration scheme, national vocational qualifications, a public information service, and professional training for practitioners. Send an SAE and 2 loose stamps, stating you would like information about a particular type of practitioner, e.g. healers, on their British Register.

National Federation of Spiritual Healers (NFSH)
Old Manor Farm Studio
Church Street
Sunbury-on-Thames
Middlesex TW16 6RG
Tel: 0891 616080 (helpline)

Provides a healer referral service for those over eighteen years of age. Phone Monday–Friday, 9 a.m. – 5 p.m.. Calls will be charged at 39p cheap rate and 49p at all other times. Or write enclosing an SAE to the above address. A wide range of books, cassettes and leaflets on healing, relaxation and other related subjects may be purchased along with the quarterly house magazine *Healing Review*.

The Spiritualist Association of Great Britain
33 Belgrave Square
London
SW1X 8QB
Tel: 0171 235 3351

The Association provides free spiritual healing seven days a week (voluntary contributions from those who can afford them are gratefully accepted). Distant healing can also be arranged. In addition, the Association offers lectures, workshops, demonstrations, private appointments with mediums and other services.

Psychic Skills
British Astrological and Psychic Society
124 Trefoilo Crescent
Broadfield
Crawley

W. Sussex
RH11 9EZ
Tel: 01293 542326

Concerned with all esoteric disciplines including mediumship, aura reading, trance, clairvoyance, astrology and numerology. Publishes a quarterly journal, available by annual subscription to non-members and free to members. Also maintains a National Register of Approved Consultants.

UFOs
British UFO Research Association (BUFORA)
1 Woodhall Drive
Batley
West Yorkshire
WF17 7SW
Tel: 01924 444049

Carries out research and educational activities and produces a number of publications. Members receive, free of charge, six issues per year of the Association's regular publication *UFO Times*. In addition, there are monthly lectures (September to June), regional meetings and every other year BUFORA co-sponsors the international UFO Conference. BUFORA also operates the 'UFOCALL' hotline that carries information about reports and updates on events (Tel: 0891 12 18 86). Calls will be charged at 39p cheap rate and 49p at all other times.

Contact International
PO Box 23

Wheatley
Oxon.
Tel: 01865 726908

Concerned with the collection of UFO reports, their systemization and analysis, and the maintenance of a UFO register containing statistics. Also publishes a quarterly magazine *Awareness* – write to the above address for subscription details.

Quest International
1st Floor
66 Boroughgate
Otley, Nr Leeds
LS21 1AE
Tel: 01943 850860

Arranges conference throughout the United Kingdom and operates an extensive UFO mail order catalogue that supplies video tapes, books, specialist reports and audio cassettes. In addition they operate a twenty-four-hour UFO report line, Tel: 01756 752216. Also produces *UFO Magazine*.

Shamanism
Eagle's Wing Centre for Contemporary Shamanism
58 Westbere Road
London NW2 3RU
Tel: 0171 435 8174

Write to the above address or telephone for information on one-day, weekend or year-long courses. The above telephone number is also a helpline and can provide information on services such as shamanic dance evenings and tapes.

171

Further Reading

General Interest

Encyclopedia of Hoaxes, Gordon Stein, Gale (USA).

The Encyclopedia of Parapsychology and Psychical Research, Arthur S. Berger, J. D., and Joyce Berger, M. A., Paragon House (USA).

Encyclopedia of the Unexplained, Jenny Randles and Peter Hough, Michael O'Mara Books Ltd, London.

Encyclopedia of the Unexplained, Magic, Occultism and Parapsychology, edited by Richard Cavendish, Arkana, London.

Explaining the Unexplained: Mysteries of the Paranormal, H. J. Eysenck and C. Sargent, Weidenfeld & Nicolson, London.

Glimpses of Reality, Linda Molton Howe, LMH Productions (USA).

The Margins of Reality, Professor Robert Jahn, Harcourt Brace & Co. Ltd, London.

Medicine, Mind and Magic, Guy Lyon Playfair, Aquarian Press, London

Natural and Supernatural, Brian Inglis, Hodder and Stoughton, London.

The Occult, Colin Wilson, Hodder and Stoughton, London.

The Oxford Companion to the Mind, edited by Richard L. Gregory, Oxford University Press, Oxford.

The Paranormal Encyclopedia, Stuart Gordon, Hodder Headline, London.

Parapsychology: The Controversial Science, R. Broughton, Rider Books, London.

The Presence of the Past, Rupert Sheldrake, Fontana, London.

Quantum Psychology, Robert Anton Wilson, Falcon.

The Reality of the Paranormal, Arthur J. Ellison, Harrap, Edinburgh.

Science and Parascience, Brian Inglis, Hodder and Stoughton, London.

Seven Experiments That Could Change the World, Rupert Sheldrake, Fourth Estate Ltd, London.

Supernature, Lyall Watson, Hodder and Stoughton, London.

World of Strange Power, Arthur C. Clarke, HarperCollins, London.

Ghosts

The Eagle and the Rose, Rosemary Altea, Bantam Press, London.

Ghost Hunter, Eddie Burks and Gillian Cribbs, Hodder Headline, London.

The Guinness Encyclopaedia of Ghosts and Spirits, Rosemary Ellen Guiley, Guinness, London.

The Haunted Pub Guide, Guy Lyon Playfair, Harrap, Edinburgh.

This House is Haunted, Guy Playfair, Souvenir Press, London.

UFOs

Abduction – Human Encounters with Aliens, John E. Mack, Simon & Schuster, London.

Above Top Secret, Timothy Good, HarperCollins, London.

Alien Liaison, Timothy Good, Arrow Books, London.

Alien Update, Timothy Good, Arrow Books, London.

Beyond Top Secret: The World-wide UFO Security Threat, Timothy Good, Sidgwick & Jackson, London

Close Encounters of the 4th Kind, C. D. B. Ryan, Weidenfeld and Nicolson, London.

Interrupted Journey, John G. Fuller, Dial Books, London.

Open Skies, Closed Minds, Nick Pope, Simon & Schuster, London.

UFOs – The Definitive Casebook, John Spencer, Hamlyn, London.

The UFO Phenomena, Edward Ashpole, Hodder Headline, London.

UFO Retrievals, Jenny Randles, Blandford Press, London.

Psychic Detectives

The Blue Sense: Psychic Detectives and Crime, Arthur Lyons and Marcello Truzzi, Mysterious Press.

Ghost of a Chance, Nella Jones, Pan Books, London.

Psychic Cop, Keith Charles, Blake Publishers, London.

The Psychic Detectives, Colin Wilson, Pan Books, London

Psychic Investigator, Harry Price, Boxtree, London.

Mental Magic (mind-reading and other psychic illusions)

Practical Mental Magic, Ted Anneman, Dover Publications.

The Big Book of Magic, Patrick Page, Breese Books.

Remote Viewing

Mind Trek, Joseph McMoneagle, Hampton Roads (USA).

Healing

Healing Now, Anthea Courtenay, J. M. Dent, London.

Theories of the Chakras, Hiroshi Motoyama, Quest Books.

Superhumans

Search in Secret Egypt, Paul Brunton, Weisler (USA).

Search in Secret India, Paul Brunton, Weisler (USA).

Shamanism

The Medicine Way, Kenneth Meadows, Element Books, Dorset.
The Shaman's Path, edited by Gary Doore, Shambala.
Shamanism, Shirley Nicholson, Quest.

Sceptic Analysis

Adventures of a Parapsychologist, Susan Blackmore, Prometheus Books.

Bizarre Beliefs, Simon Hoggart and Mike Hutchinson, Richard Cohen Books, London.

Guidelines for Testing Psychic Claimants, Richard Wiseman and Robert L. Morris, University of Hertfordshire Press, Hatfield.

The Hundredth Monkey and Other Paradigms of the Paranormal, edited by Kendrick Frasier, Prometheus Books.

Psychic Sleuths, edited by Joe Nickell, Hodder Headline, London.

Science: Good, Bad and Bogus, Martin Gardener, Prometheus Books.

UFOs – The Public Deceived, Philip J. Klass, Prometheus Books.

Magazines

The Fortean Times
20 Paul Street
Frome
Somerset
BA11 1DX
Tel: 01373 451777

Monthly magazine available through leading stockists. Alternatively, telephone or write to the above address for services including subscriptions, general enquiries and books.

Kindred Spirit
Foxhold
Dartington
Totnes
Devon
TQ9 6EB
Tel: 01803 866686

A quarterly magazine that may be subscribed to or obtained through specialist book shops and some natural whole food shops. It is also possible to order through your local newsagent.

New Age
PO Box 1947
Marion
OH 43306 2047
USA

Bimonthly magazine available mainly in specialist book shops. Write to the above address for a sample copy and subscription details.

Nexus
55 Queens Road
East Grinstead
West Sussex
RH19 1BG
Tel: 01342 322854

Bimonthly magazine available mainly, although not exclusively, through specialist book shops. Write to the address above for subscription details.

Psychic News
Clock Cottage
Britten House
Stansted Hall
Stansted
Essex CM24 8UD
Tel: 01279 817050

Weekly magazine available, by order, through most leading stockists. Alternatively, telephone the above number for services including subscriptions, general enquiries and books.

The Sacred Hoop
28 Cowl Street
Evesham
Worcestershire
WR11 4PL
Tel: 01386 49680

Obtainable in some new age shops. Telephone the above number for subscription details. Alternatively, send an A4 envelope with two first-class stamps to receive a sample copy.

The Skeptic
PO Box 475
Manchester
M60 2TH

Bimonthly magazine available by subscription only. Write to the above address for a free sample issue.

The Skeptical Enquirer
10 Crescent View
Loughton
Essex
IG10 4PZ
Tel: 0181 508 2989

Magazine offering critical analysis on subjects including the paranormal, pseudo-science and the frontiers of science. Available by subscription only from the above address.

UFO Magazine
1st Floor, 66 Boroughgate
Otley
Near Leeds
LS21 1AE
Tel: 01943 850860

Bimonthly magazine available from many leading stockists. Alternatively, telephone the above number for services including subscriptions, general enquiries, UFO Directory orders, conference tickets, information news desk and classified and place advertisements.

Specialist Book Shops
Anglo American Books
Tel: 01267 211880

Arcturus
47 Fore Street
Totnes
Devon
TQ9 5NI
Tel: 01803 864363

Compendium Bookshop
234 Camden High Street
London NW1 8QS
Tel: 0171 485 8944

Enigma
100 Old Christchurch Road
Bournemouth
Dorset
BH1 1LR
Tel: 01202 316454

Mysteries
9–11 Monmouth Street
London WC2H 9DA
Tel: 0171 240 3688

The Sorcerer's Apprentice (Mail Order Only)
6–8 Burley Lodge Road
Leeds
LS6 1QP
Tel: 01132 451309

Watkins Bookshop (and Mail Order Department)
19 Cecil Court
Charing Cross Road
London WC2N 4EZ
Tel: 0171 836 2182

Index

African shamans
(*sangomas*), 141–3
Agannis, Harry, 3
Aikido, 161–2
aliens
animal mutilations, 49–50,
51–4
Area 51, 36, 38
and Brookings Institution, 45
claim of co-operation between
US Government and, 36–7,
55–6
discovery of at Roswell, 32–3
use of radiation, 54–5
see also UFOs
Allison, Dorothy, 58–63
Altea, Rosemary, 10–15, 22–3,
59, 138
animal mutilations, 37, 47–54
alien theory, 49–50, 51–4
theories explaining, 49–52
animals
psychic abilities of, 98–102
Area 51, 36–9, 41, 42–3
Association for the Scientific
Study of Anomalous
Phenomena, The, 165
athletes
and 'the zone', 155–7
aurora borealis, 28

baby Abbie, abduction of, 72–3
Balint, Michael, 135
Beasant, Malcolm, 83, 139–40
Beijing Evening News, 114
Belgium
UFO sightings, 25–6
Birin, Captain V., 28
'black projects', 42–3
blue tits, 98–9, 102
Bohr, Niels, 162
Boshier, Adrian, 144
brain, human, 162
Braud, William, 2–3, 155
Brazel, William, 31, 32
Brennan, Lesley, 88
British Astrological and Psychic
Society, 169–70
British Complementary
Medicine Association,
167–8
British Premonitions Bureau, 89
British UFO Research
Association
(BUFORA), 170
Brookings Institution, 44–5
Browne, Robert Charles, 63
Buchanan, Joseph, 70–1
Burks, Eddie, 10, 15–20, 138
Butterfly nightclub
(Oldham), 8–9
Byrd, Dr Randolph, 136

Camelot, 105
card-guessing test, 76–7, 79–80
Cash, Betty, 54–6
cats, 100
channelling, 5–7
Cheyenne American Indian
    tribe, 91
chi, 157–61
China
    research into 'Z's abilities, 113
Christianity, 7
Church, Heather, 63
clairvoyance, 64, 73, 77 *see also*
    psychic detectives
Clarke, Ben, 140
'cold' reading, 95–7
collective unconscious, 79
Conan Doyle, Arthur, 72
Contact International, 170–1
Cousins, Norman, 136–40
Coutt's Bank, 16

Dawson, Elizabeth, 151
De Brouwer, Colonel
    Wilfried, 26
Denham, Irene and Paul, 12
di Padua, Gerald, 143–4
Di Piertro, Vincent, 44
Dickens, Charles, 1
Dinsdale, Peter, 69
dogs
    healing of Sasha, 139–40
    JT and telepathy, 99–100
dreams, 82–3, 91–2
Duggan, Sheila and Larry,
    19–20

Eagle and the Rose, The
    (Altea) 14–15

Edwards, William, 13
energy healing, 130–1, 139–40
ESP (Extrasensory
    Perception), 76–7, 79, 82,
    83, 85, 107
    defined, 64
    percentage experience, 76
    studies into by Rhine, 79–81
    see also telepathy
Estabany, Oskar, 146
Everett, Carol, 72–3
Extraterrestrial Biological
    Entities (EBEs) *see* aliens

faith, 108, 132
First World War
    telepathic precognition, 79
Flixborough plant disaster, 88–9
fraud, 115–18
Freud, Sigmund, 78–9

Gaia theory, 162
Ganzfeld test, 81–5, 89–90, 91
Gasparetto, Luis Antonio, 5
Geller, Uri, 114–16, 117–18
General Extrasensory Perception
    (GESP), 64, 77
ghosts, 1–23
    channelling, 5–7
    communication with, 14–15
    difficulty in defining, 4–5
    difficulty in researching, 9
    experience of Rosemary
        Altea, 10–16, 22, 59, 138
    famous people's encounters
        with, 2–3
    investigation into by Eddie
        Burks, 10, 15–20, 138
    sightings by widows, 2, 21–2

studies on numbers
  experiencing, 1–2
theories explaining, 7–9
untrapping of spirits by
  love, 18, 20–21, 138
Girard, Jean-Pierre, 118
Giza sphinx, 46
Goldman Air Base
  (Kentucky), 33–4, 35
Grad, Professor Bernard, 146
Great Train Robbery, 58
Grey, Duncan, 72–3
Guitar Player, The (Vermeer),
  66–7

Haines, Dr Richard, 24
Hamilton, Alexander, 53
Hansel, Mark, 88–91
Hasted, Professor John, 116,
  118–20
healing, x, 130–50
  experiments into the psychic
    and, 146–48
  and faith, 135–9
  laying on of hands, 139–40
  and morphic fields, 148
  and power of love, 138
  psychic surgery, 143–4
  and psychokinesis, 147–8
  and religion, 135, 138–9
  remote, 148
  sangomas, 144–5
  Shamanism, 141–3
Health Watch, 168
Herbert, Benson, 112
Hindu mystics, 82
Hoagland, Richard, 43–4, 45
'holistic' approach, x–xi
Honorton, Charles, 81–5, 89

'hot' reading, 94
houses
  feelings associated with, 71
Howard, Thomas, Duke of
  Norfolk, 16
Howe, Linda Moulton, 48
Hunt, Mike, 37
Hyman, Ray, 84

Ignatenko, Professor Albert,
  77–8
Institute for Complementary
  Medicine, 168
Institute of Space-Medical
  Engineering (ISME), 113,
  114
Introduction to Psychology, 85

Jahn, Robert, 122, 123
Joanne, 18, 19
Jones, Nella, 57, 58, 65–72
  early psychic abilities, 65–6
  theft of Vermeer's painting
    case, 66–7
  Yorkshire Ripper case, 68–9
JT (dog), 99–100
Jung, Carl, 79, 91

Knapp, George, 41–2
Kulagina, Nina, 110–12

Landrum, Vickie, 54–5
Lavrinenko, Valeri, 77–8, 152–5
laying on of hands, 139–40
Lazar, Robert, 38–42
Lear, John, 36, 37
Lill, John, 5
love
  and healing, 138

untrapping of spirits by, 20–
21, 138

McMonengle, Joe, 46–7, 85–7
magicians, 93–4, 116, 117
Maimonides Community Health
Center, 82–3
Malzev, General Igor, 28
Mantell, Thomas, 34
Marcel, Major Jesse, 32
Marchioness, 17
Mars
Cydonia pyramids, 45–6,
46–8
identification of human
face, 43–4, 45, 46
martial arts, 157–61
mass consciousness, 124–5
Maxwell, Terry, 11
metal-bending, 114–15, 118–19
micro-PK, ix–x, 108, 120–4
Mind Sciences Foundation, 147
Moore, Roger, 2
morphic fields, 101–3, 138, 148
Myers, W. H., 78

NASA, 43, 44, 45, 47
National Federation of Spiritual
Healers (NFSH), 169
National Lottery, 105, 124
National Opinion Research
Council, 2
near-death experience
(NDE), 86
New York Times, 45
Newton, Isaac, 104
Nikolic, Seka, 130–1
Ninja, 160
Ninjitsu, 160

North Dakota
UFO sighting, 34
Novak, Kim, 2–3

O. J. Simpson trial, 125
orgone energy accumulator, 137
orthodox medicine, 131–2, 140–
1, 149
osteopathy, 149

paranormal
change in view of, 57
defined, vii
Pearce, Hubert, 81
pigeons, 98, 99, 102
PK *see* psychokinesis
placebo effect, 132–6, 143
Poe, Edgar Allan, 1
Polish boy incident, 60–2
possession, 7
premonition *see* precognition
precognition, 75, 76, 87–91
during First World War, 79
scepticism over, 91–2
testing for, 89–90, 121–2
Princeton Engineering
Anomalies (PEAR)
project, 122–3
Project Blue Book, 35, 36
Project Sign, 35
psychic abilities
difficulty in defining, 76–7
psychic detection
origins and nature, 71–2
psychic detectives, 57–74
Carol Everett, 72–3
and legal cases, 72–3
police's reluctance to
acknowledge, 70–2

see also Allison, Dorothy;
    Jones, Nella
psychic surgery, 143–4
psychokinesis (PK), 76, 79,
    104–29
  definition, 64–5, 104–5
  experiments conducted by
    Toronto Society for
    Psychical Research, 108–9
  experiments into effects of
    mass consciousness, 124–6
  and fraud, 116–17
  and healing, 147–8
  metal bending, 114–15,
    118–19
  'micro', ix–x, 108, 120–4
  National Lottery
    experiment, 105
  Nina Kulagina, 110–12
  and quantum physics, 63,
    104, 106–7, 127–9
  and random mechanical
    cascade experiment, 122–3
  Schmidt's experiments,
    126–9
  Uri Geller, 114–18
  'Z', 113–14
psychometry, 71
Psychophysical Research
    Laboratories
    (Princeton), 83

quantum physics, 8, 101, 162
  and psychokinesis, 63, 104,
    106–7, 127–9
  and telepathy, 90
Quest International, 171

radiation

  alien use of, 54–5
Radin, Dean, 89–90, 124–6
Randi, James, 97, 115
Random mechanical cascade
    (RMC), 122–3
random number generator
    (RNG), 120
Reagan, Ronald, 42–3
Reich, Dr Wilhelm, 137
religion
  and channelling, 7
  and healing, 135, 138–9
  and telepathy, 78
remote healing, 148
remote viewing, 85–7
research laboratories, 166
rheumatoid arthritis, 130
Rhine, J. B., 79–80, 99
Roberts, Jane, 5–6
Roland, Ian, 94
Rosenthal, Robert, 85
Rossi, Ernest, 137
Roswell (New Mexico)
  UFO evidence at, 30–3, 36
Russell, Peter, 162

sangomas, 144–5
Sasha (dog), 139–40
Saurbacher, Professor Robert, 33
Savalas, Telly, 3
Schlugen, Brigadier-General, 35
Schmidt, Helmut, 120–2, 126–9
science, 57, 104, 161, 163
Scott, Christopher, 85, 91–2
Semyenchenko, Lieutenant-
    Colonel A., 27–8
Seth, 5–6, 21
Shamanism, 137, 141–3, 171, 175
Shaolin monks, ix, 160

Sheldrake, Rupert, 75–6, 98–102, 138, 148
siddhi, 82
Sirisena, Ananda, 45–6
Society for Psychical Research, 1–2, 78, 165–6
Soviet Union, 30
  UFO sightings, 27–9
Spiritualist Association of Great Britain, The, 169
Stealth technology, 42
staring, ix, 75–6
Stevens, Lieutenant-Colonel Wendelle, 37–8
Strategic Defense Initiative, 42–3
Strontium-90 isotope, 120–1
superhumans, 151–61
Sutcliffe, Peter, 68–9

Taylor, Professor John, 116
Taylor, Shaw, 85, 86–7
telepathy, 75–103
  and animals, 98–102
  deceptions used in readings, 93–7
  definition, 64, 75
  history of concept, 78–9
  and love, 138
  and medical profession, 78–9
  and morphic fields, 101–3
  precognition *see* precognition
  and quantum physics, 90
  and religion, 78
  'remote viewing', 85–7
  similarities with martial arts, 159
  tests into, 79–85
termites, 98, 102
Topen, Gordon, 72

Toronto Society for Psychical Research, 108–10
Torrey, E. F., 141
Tower of London, 1

Ueshiba, Morihei, 160–1
UFOs (unidentified flying objects), 24–56
  Area 51, 36–9, 42–3
  description of by Lazar, 39–42
  evidence of crash wreckage at Roswell, 30–3, 36
  Goldman Air Base incident, 33–4, 35
  official secrecy over, 29–30, 33, 35–6, 44, 47
  sightings in Belgium (1989–90), 25–6
  sightings in former Soviet Union, 27–9
  taken seriously by military personnel, 24–5, 34–5, 42
  US policy towards, 35–6
  use of weaponry against, 42–3
  see also aliens
University of Nevada, 148

Valdez, Gabriel, 52, 53, 54
Vandenberg, General, 35
Vermeer painting theft, 73–4
Viking, 66–7
voodoo healing ritual, 148

Wales
  crushing of school by avalanche (1966), 87–8
War of the Worlds, The (radio broadcast), 30

'warm' reading, 94–5
Welles, Orson, 30
'will to live', viii–ix
Wiseman, Richard, 93–4
Workers' Tribune, The, 27–8

Yorkshire Ripper case, 68–9

'Z', (Zang Baozheng), 113–14
'zone, the', 155–7

faber and faber

The Hypnotic World of Paul McKenna

Television's hypnotic sensation shows you how to create success!

Paul McKenna demonsrates how hypnosis can be used for a whole range of practical and therapeutic purposes. You'll soon be able to understand exactly what hypnosis is and how it can work for you.

This step-by-step approach will enable you to boost your energy, control stress and achieve greater results in many other areas of your life.

faber and faber

Paul McKenna

Please send me:

____ copies of **The Hypnotic World of Paul McKenna**

(0 571 16802 7) £5.99 each

I enclose a cheque for £ _____

made payable to Faber and Faber Ltd.

Please charge my:

Access / Visa / Amex / Diner's Club / Eurocard / Switch

(Switch Issue Number _____)

Name of Cardholder _____ Expiry Date: _____

Account Number:

☐ ☐ ☐ ☐ ☐ ☐ ☐ ☐ ☐ ☐ ☐ ☐ ☐ ☐ ☐ ☐

Name _____

Address _____

Signed _____Date _____

Send to:

Faber Book Services,

Burnt Mill, Elizabeth Way, Harlow, Essex CM20 2HX

Tel 01279 417134 Fax 01279 417366